HOW TO STUDY THE BIBLE

BRYAN MEADOWS

How to Study the Bible

Bryan Meadows

www.bryanmeadows.com
bryan@embassychurchatl.com

Published by Embassy Advantage™

Cover Design by Jason Long

Editing Team:
Vanessa Hunter
Tiffany Buckner

Research Team:
Tiffany Buckner
Glenda Giles

ISBN: 978-1-7348612-2-8

Unless otherwise noted, Scripture quotations are taken from The Holy Bible, New King James Version® (NKJV). Copyright© 1982 by Thomas Nelson. Used by permission. All rights reserved.

Table of Contents

Getting Started

Welcome to a renewed way of viewing and studying the Bible. Here's a fact to get started with: you can only apply what you understand. Anything outside of the realm of understanding is called chance; in other words, what you're essentially doing is gambling with the Word. You're tossing it like a pair of dice, hoping that you'll get lucky, and this mode of study and application creates doubt, religiousness and a works mentality. This is why I created How to Study the Bible! My objective is to help you find the style of biblical study and application that works best for you.

Over the course of time, people have attempted to study the Bible using the same format of reading and comprehension that was taught to them in school. The problem with this is …not everyone learns the same way. Additionally, our educational system taught us to memorize, but not necessarily understand words, numbers and facts. So, we can readily identify the words on a page, but most of us don't have full comprehension of what we're reading. This is why it's so easy for us to read one verse in the Bible and completely forget what we've just read in a matter of minutes! The Bible tells us to meditate on the Word of God. What this means is that God wants us to take His Word into our minds, and then, transfer it into our hearts through a series of study, meditation and prayer. He also wants us to attend our local assemblies so that we can get a greater understanding of, not only what He said, but why He said it. Without the "why," understanding is impossible to attain.

How to Study the Bible is a book designed to aid you in the study and application of the Word of God. In this guide, I've extracted many biblical facts from the Bible and other resources, and I've compiled them here so that you can take the information and revelation from the pages and transfer it to your memory bank. From there, you can withdraw and apply it whenever you need to.

How to Use this Guide

This book is filled with biblical facts that have been extracted for you to study. To get started, make sure that you have your Bible ready and an apparatus like a pen, notepad, phone or computer in front of you. Also, you will need:

1. To find a quiet space in your home or wherever you plan to study. Make sure you're not distracted by anything or anyone.
2. Choose the best time of day to start your Bible study. For many people, the best time to study is when the members of their household are asleep.
3. Create a welcoming atmosphere in your home or place of study. Note: one of the

reasons some people find it hard to study the Bible is because they attempt to do so in chaotic environments. They are either surrounded by junk, bills, pictures or something that keeps serving as a distraction. This is why many people in the older generation literally had prayer closets. They used this space to pray and to study so that they could escape all the things and the people that would command their attention.

4. Use a fresh notebook or create a new document on your phone or computer to take notes; this is so that you don't have trouble locating these notes whenever you sit down to study.
5. Write down anything that you have trouble memorizing or anything that stands out to you and study it. Utilize Google (or whatever search engine you prefer), along with your Bible.
6. Every time you sit down to read more of this book, be sure to go over what you learned the day prior.
7. Test your knowledge! Use the worksheets at the back of this book to test your knowledge! Test your knowledge after reading a chapter, take that same test the next day to ensure that you've remembered what you learned the day prior and test yourself once a week on everything you've learned that week.
8. Apply what you've learned! Application takes the information and marries it with your belief system. In other words, it helps you to remember what you've learned.

Common Mistakes

As in all things, there is a wrong way and a right way to study the Bible. Below, you'll find a few mistakes that people commonly make.

1. **Studying with the wrong motive!** If your goal is to learn the Word so that you can appear to be smart, you will find it difficult to commit to a regular study schedule. All the same, you'll gather knowledge, but no understanding, which is the very backdrop of religion. Second Timothy 2:15 says it this way, “Study to shew thyself approved unto God, a workman that needeth not to be ashamed, rightly dividing the word of truth.” Why should I study? To show myself approved! Am I trying to get approved for Heaven? No. What then am I applying for? The answer is, I'm studying so that I can withdraw whatever it is that I need from Heaven whenever I need it. In order for God to approve this withdrawal, He has to see faith. And of course, faith comes by hearing, and hearing by the Word of God. In other words, I have to know what the Word says, apply what the Word says (faith without works is dead) and believe what the Word says. And my motive must be to glorify God, not myself!
2. **Studying at the wrong time.** We have synced our bodies and our minds to our environments, atmospheres and schedules. And now, we have to incorporate true Bible

study (not just Bible reading) to our daily schedules. To do this, we have to find the time that works best for us individually. For example, early in the morning is a great time to study the Bible, BUT if you have a habit of getting up late and rushing to get to work, it goes without saying that mornings are not the best time for you to study. This is because if you attempt to study the Word in the morning, you will read the scriptures, instead of studying the Word (the person of Jesus Christ). So maybe the best time for you to study is on your lunch break or at home before you go to bed. Then again, some people study their Bibles outside their homes while in their cars, normally after they've returned home from work. They literally pull into their driveways and start studying! Again, you have to find what works best for you!

3. **Having no study plan.** It is always a great idea to know what, where and when to study. One way of doing this is to start where you left off OR to study a specific subject like tithing, fear or faith. If you are going to study this way, you'd have to search online for scriptures on whatever it is that you're studying about.
4. **Being inconsistent.** Inconsistency disallows you from creating a habit of reading the Bible. This allows you to be led by your emotions and your personal schedule, thus, causing you to subject God to your timing and feelings, and not the other way around. Create a schedule and study the Bible consistently every day at that time. It typically takes 17-21 days to establish a habit, so this is something you want to do daily until it becomes a must-do or a habit for you.
5. **Studying when you're tired!** The average American likes to wind down before reading/studying the Bible! This can be good for some, but for most people, it doesn't necessarily work well because your mind will want to do what your body is doing—it will want to relax! Sure, go somewhere and get comfortable, but don't wait until you've poured yourself out all day long, taken your shower and climbed into bed before reading the Bible. Study when your mind is fully alert and ready to learn! Note: we often overindulge in the information we find on social media when, in truth, whenever we find ourselves tempted to go on social media, we should (instead) open our Bibles and study. After we're done, we can give what's left of our attention to social media.
6. **Mystifying the Bible.** A lot of believers have no arranged order in which they study the Bible, so consequently, they flip through the pages and read the page that opens up for them. They believe that by doing this, they are prophetically reading what God wants them to read, not realizing that this is okay sometimes, but it is NOT the way to study the Word. The mystification of God has called many believers to search out the mysteries of God without having a revelation of God through His Word. What this means is, they want the deep things, but not the foundation. This mode of “study” only leads believers to become more mystical, emotional and impractical in their application of the Word.

BOOKS OF THE BIBLE

Genesis	Exodus	Leviticus	Numbers	Deuteronomy	Joshua
Judges	Ruth	1 Samuel	2 Samuel	1 Kings	2 Kings
1 Chronicles	2 Chronicles	Ezra	Nehemiah	Esther	Job
Psalms	Proverbs	Ecclesiastes	Solomon	Isaiah	Jeremiah
Lamentations	Ezekiel	Daniel	Hosea	Joel	Amos
Obadiah	Jonah	Micah	Nahum	Habakkuk	Zephaniah
Haggai	Zechariah	Malachi	Matthew	Mark	Luke
John	Acts	Romans	1 Corinthians	2 Corinthians	Galatians
Ephesians	Philippians	Colossians	1 Thessalonians	2 Thessalonians	1 Timothy
2 Timothy	Titus	Philemon	Hebrews	James	1 Peter
2 Peter	1 John	2 John	3 John	Jude	Revelation

Styles of Study

There are many styles of studying the Bible, but below, I'll detail three main styles, all of which I've named to help you memorize your particular style. Try them all to see what works best for you.

The Sprinkle Maneuver

This approach is for believers who are easily distracted and find it hard to study the Word in one setting. Before I detail the steps to studying the Bible using this method, let me say this—you can graduate from one style of study to another. If you're young in the faith, chances are, you may have to start with the Sprinkle Maneuver, but the goal is for you to gain control over your mind so that you can eventually become attracted to the Word and learn to study the Word more thoroughly, intentionally and intensively.

To apply the Sprinkle maneuver, follow these steps:

1. Choose what book and chapter of the Bible you plan to study throughout the day on every given day.
2. Look to see how many verses are in that particular chapter and divide that number by four. The reason you need to do this is because you're going to stretch your Bible study time out over the course of four hours. So, for example, if you're reading John 1, which has 50 verses, you'd divide 50 by four. The answer is 12.5, so you'd read 12 verses every hour or every other hour, and 14 verses in your last setting. And don't just

read each scripture, study and meditate on the Word. Reading engages your reading comprehension, as taught to you in school. This can prove to be relatively ineffective when studying the Bible. Instead, study each scripture by (1) repeating it several times, and (2) studying the key words within each verse.

3. At the end of the day, read the book of your choice in its entirety. This is to refresh your memory and to stabilize your attention span.

The Immersion Maneuver

This is the study style that most believers practice, and hear me—if this style does not work for you, do NOT feel pressured to adopt it as your own. Over time, you will find the study style that best suits you!

Immersion is as it sounds. Think of a bath. When a person is placed in a bathtub or sits in a bathtub, that person's head is above the water; this is called immersion. Please note that the head represents authority. In this style of study, what you're basically doing is reading a book of the Bible in its entirety, but running each verse of scripture through your mind until you either remember the verse in its entirety or you remember some of the key words in the verse. What you'll also need to do is study those key words or any words that stick out to you. Also, engage your mind by activating each verse. For example, let's look at John 14, which reads, "The Word became flesh and made his dwelling among us. We have seen his glory, the glory of the one and only Son, who came from the Father, full of grace and truth."

The Word (keyword) became flesh (keyword) and made His dwelling among us. To better understand this, I would first study scriptures about the Word, for example, John 1:1, Revelation 19:3 and Hebrews 4:12. Next, I'd move on to flesh, and I'd start with the making of the first Adam (Genesis 2:7). I'd then study the works of the flesh (Galatians 5:19-21). What I'm able to extract from this so far is that the Word (Jesus) stepped into the sin nature of a human and overcame the flesh; that is, the temptations. This would lead me to Hebrews 2:18, which reads, "For since He Himself was tempted in that which He has suffered, He is able to come to the aid of those who are tempted."

The Submersion Maneuver

When someone is submerged in water, that person's entire body, including his or her head, is under the water. The person is hidden and only the water can be seen. This is when you bathe or, better yet, drown yourself in the Word! Using this style of learning, you'd create a rigorous study schedule where you'd read the Bible two to three times a day (at minimum) for a period of one or more hours. You'd use sticky notes to post up scriptures all around your house so that everywhere you look, you will see the Word of God. And of course, people who use this method post up scriptures in their workplaces, in their cars and just about every place they frequent.

This approach is designed to submerge the student in scriptures, thus, forcing the student to see and study the Word, even when he or she goes, for example, to the refrigerator or to the bathroom. This is really effective when you post up notes in the rooms that you frequent the most. Some people even go to sleep with a Bible app playing on their phones so that they can subliminally implant the scriptures into their memories. And of course, some believers would say that this method is "too extreme," but that's just their opinion. Not everyone is a student of the Word; some people are visitors, meaning, they visit the scriptures, but they don't necessarily take them in their hearts with them. If you are a student, you need to immerse or submerge yourself in the Word of God.

HERMENEUTICS

A Brief Look at Hermeneutics

What is hermeneutics, and why is it important? Encyclopedia Britannica offers an answer to these questions. It reads, "Hermeneutics, the study of the general principles of biblical interpretation. For both Jews and Christians throughout their histories, the primary purpose of hermeneutics, and of the exegetical methods employed in interpretation, has been to discover the truths and values of the Bible."

The words "hermeneutics" and "exegeses" are oftentimes used interchangeably, but hermeneutics is a broader scope of exegetics because it deals with written, verbal and non-verbal communication, whereas, exegesis deals primarily with written text. There are three styles of hermeneutics. Look at the chart below to get an understanding.

Literal Interpretation	Moral Interpretation	Allegorical Interpretation
This approach takes the biblical text word-for-word, giving no room for prophetical utterances, parables or any other translations. A lot of the biblical text is literal, but some of it is allegorical or metaphorical. The Bible was not written for mankind to "understand". It was literally written for the believer; its many mysteries can only be understood by Spirit-filled believers to whom understanding has been granted!	This approach deals primarily with ethics. The goal here is to read between the lines to extrapolate the moral lesson behind each story or scripture, and how to apply what was extracted to our everyday lives.	This approach deals more with symbolism. For example, the Church is allegorically understood to be the Bride of Christ, Jerusalem is used to allegorically represent Heaven, etc. The allegorical approach is designed to take what people understand (natural things) and use it as a reference point to help them better understand spiritual things.

None of these approaches are wrong; this is why you have to be led by the Spirit of God, and not allow pride to tempt you into giving an answer when you don't have a foundation for that answer. As you venture further into this guide, you will see examples of all three styles of teaching/learning.

THE BOOKS OF THE BIBLE

If you ever want to memorize the scriptures or master the text, the best practice is to first commit the books of the Bible to memory! This creates a mental filing system for every scripture so, for example, if someone mentions the healing power of the blood of Jesus, they will trigger your mind's filtering system. Without you putting much thought into it, a book will suddenly pop up in your mind. Initially, you may find yourself saying, “There's a scripture about healing in the book of Isaiah, I think.” Over time, you'll come to remember that one of the scriptures referencing healing is Isaiah 53:5. This will help you to better memorize the scriptural text as well!

Below, I've compiled a complete list of the books of the Bible! Commit this information to memory. You can do this using several methodologies. They are:

1. **Verbal and/or Mental Repetition.** Using this method, you just repeatedly say the words in order, for example, you can start off memorizing the first five books. You'd say their names over and over again until you've memorized them. Then, you'd memorize the next five. You'd do this until you've successfully committed the books to memory!
2. **The Song Technique:** Using this method, you'd simply commit the books to memory by making a song out of their names similar to the alphabet song! Find a beat, a rhythm and/or a harmony, and find a way to creatively interweave the song into the sound!
3. **The Alphabet Extraction Method:** This method is a little more complex, but it's effective for some learners. Using this method, you'd simply write down the first letter of every book of the Bible in order. You'd then remember the alphabets or create names wherever you see vowels. You can even toss a few scriptural words in the mix. For example, the first eight books' alphabets are GELNDJJR. If I wanted to remember these, I could say Gel, ND-Double-J, R. If I wanted to add 1st and 2nd Samuel to the mix, I'd follow it up with Double Sam or Sam, Sam. Again, this method is more complex, but it actually works for people who are heavy thinkers or, better yet, people who find basic repetition too monotonous or mundane to commit to.
4. **The Alphabet Song Method:** This is a hybrid of the Song Method and the Alphabet Extraction Method! Like the Alphabet Extraction Method, the Alphabet Song Method requires you to write down the first letter of every book of the Bible in order. After this, you'd simply make an alphabet song using each letter. Don't forget to find a rhythm for the song, or you can go online and find a beat to commit the song to.
5. **The Standard Method:** Used by most people, this methodology encourages you to write down each book of the Bible and study those names every day. This method is the most effective, but it also takes the most time.
6. **Name Association Technique:** Associate each first letter with the name of someone you know! I gave an example of this method below!

7. **Create your own technique or search online for other memorization tools.** You are as unique as your fingerprint, so you may have to create or find a technique that's best suited for you. Look at your patterns. What is your style of learning? Apply that style!

Name Association Technique

I've recorded the first letter of every book in the Old Testament. Note: You can use this list for any other method you choose to use.

G	E	L	N	D	J	J	R	1-S	2-S	1-K	2-K	1-C
2-C	E	N	E	J	P	P	E	SS	I	J	L	E
D	H	J	A	O	J	M	N	H	Z	H	Z	M

Using the Name Association Technique, I'd commit each of these letters to memory by associating them with a name. For example, look at the list I created below.

Greg	Edward	Larry	Nigel	David	Jerry	John	Robert
1st Sam	2nd Sam	1st Karen	2nd Karen	1st Cory	2nd Cory	Erica	Nathan
Emily	Jason	Patrick	Paul	Emory	Sam Short	Isaac	Joe
Lisa	Evan	Donald	Hank	Jack	Arthur	Oliver	Justin
Michael	Nancy	Howard	Zelma	Haley	Zachary	Martin	

This technique seems complicated at first, but it's actually very effective! You can simplify it by, for example, associating two names with one another like a first and a surname. Examples: Greg Edward, Larry Nigel, David Jerry and John Robert

Please note that you can combine some of the aforementioned techniques as well.

39 Books in the Old Testament

Genesis	Exodus	Leviticus
Numbers	Deuteronomy	Joshua
Judges	Ruth	1st Samuel
2nd Samuel	1st Kings	2nd Kings

1st Chronicles	2nd Chronicles	Ezra
Nehemiah	Esther	Job
Psalms	Proverbs	Ecclesiastes
Song of Solomon	Isaiah	Jeremiah
Lamentations	Ezekiel	Daniel
Hosea	Joel	Amos
Obadiah	Jonah	Micah
Nahum	Habakkuk	Zephaniah
Haggai	Zechariah	Malachi

27 Books of the New Testament

Matthew	Mark	Luke
John	Acts of the Apostles	Romans
First Corinthians	Second Corinthians	Galatians
Ephesians	Philippians	Colossians
First Thessalonians	Second Thessalonians	First Timothy
Second Timothy	Titus	Philemon
Hebrews	James	First Peter
Second Peter	First John	Second John
Third John	Jude	Revelations

Books of the Old Testament by Category

Pentateuch	Historical	Poetical	Prophetic
Genesis	Joshua	Jobs	Isaiah
Exodus	Judges	Psalms	Jeremiah
Leviticus	Ruth	Proverbs	Lamentations
Numbers	1 Samuel	Ecclesiastes	Ezekiel

Pentateuch	Historical	Poetical	Prophetic
Deuteronomy	2 Samuel	Songs of Solomon	Daniel
	1 Kings		Hosea
	2 Kings		Joel
	1 Chronicles		Amos
	2 Chronicles		Obadiah
	Ezra		Jonah
	Nehemiah		Micah
	Esther		Nahum
			Habakkuk
			Zephaniah
			Haggai
			Zechariah
			Malachi

STUDY AND SHOW YOURSELF APPROVED

THE PROPHETS OF THE BIBLE

Major and Minor Prophets of the Bible

Note: The major Prophets are shaded in gray.

Isaiah	Jeremiah	Lamentations
Ezekiel	Hosea	Daniel
Joel	Amos	Obadiah
Jonah	Micah	Nahum
Habakkuk	Zephaniah	Haggai
Zechariah		Malachi

Prophetesses Mentioned in the Bible

Miriam Exodus 15:20	**Huldah** 2 Kings 22:14	**Anna** Luke 2:36-38
Deborah Judges 4:4	**Isaiah's Wife** Isaiah 8:3	**Philip's Four Daughters** Acts 21:8-9

Old Testament Prophets (List)

Prophets	Era	Scriptures
Jonah	810-790 BC	2 Kings 13-14
Joel	790-760 BC	2 Kings 11-15
Amos	780-760 BC	2 Kings 14-15
Hosea	785-725 BC	2 Kings 15-18
Isaiah	750-695 BC	2 Kings 15-20
Micah	745-725 BC	2 Kings 15
Nahum	660-630 BC	2 Kings 15-18
Zephaniah	630-620 BC	Isaiah 10
Habakkuk	620-610 BC	2 Kings 23

Prophets	Era	Scriptures
Jeremiah	628-588 BC	2 Kings 22-25
Daniel	606-534 BC	2 Kings 23-25
Obadiah	587 BC	2 Kings 25
Ezekiel	596-574 BC	2 Kings 24
Haggai	520-518 BC	Ezra 5-6
Zechariah	520-510 BC	Ezra 5-6
Malachi	420-397 BC	Nehemiah 13

Major and Minor Prophets of the Bible

G	M	W	F	D	M	Q	O	C	R	B	E	H	H	J	D	B
W	G	N	V	Z	D	T	P	K	H	I	T	A	N	C	L	G
T	J	E	G	O	W	W	O	D	O	N	I	G	A	W	P	U
Z	J	R	A	Y	B	W	H	A	B	A	K	K	U	K	S	W
Q	D	S	H	V	V	A	D	X	S	H	B	S	L	Z	G	U
L	X	F	X	F	A	S	D	I	J	U	O	G	A	S	C	X
Z	P	I	Z	C	N	D	D	I	O	M	O	X	M	L	T	A
N	O	A	S	A	R	M	A	L	A	C	H	I	E	Z	F	B
P	V	J	B	D	T	G	V	N	Y	H	E	I	N	E	J	P
X	B	U	H	G	G	N	E	U	I	N	K	V	T	C	S	G
H	O	S	E	A	N	E	J	E	R	E	M	I	A	H	E	J
Q	Z	Z	H	M	J	P	O	O	Z	N	L	B	T	A	I	E
F	G	W	I	S	I	F	E	E	N	K	E	H	I	R	V	Z
S	H	U	F	W	W	C	L	R	F	A	X	P	O	I	V	X
Z	J	E	Z	E	P	H	A	N	I	A	H	Y	N	A	E	A
A	K	Z	M	D	A	G	I	H	L	V	P	H	S	H	B	G
I	E	R	J	F	U	N	S	W	V	L	P	J	J	W	Z	N

Amos
Daniel
Ezekiel
Habakkuk
Haggai
Hosea
Isaiah
Jeremiah
Joel
Jonah
Lamentations
Malachi
Micah
Nahum
Obadiah
Zechariah
Zephaniah

UNDERSTANDING THE WORD OF GOD

When we hear or see the morpheme "word," we normally think of a group of alphabetical characters brought together to create a single expression. And it is for this reason that when we hear Jesus referenced as the Word of God, we typically don't try to understand what God is saying about the Christ. Instead, we settle it within our hearts as a mystery that has been solved just enough for us to embrace it, but distant enough for us to wonder about it. It is human nature to take a question mark and turn it into an exclamation point in order to settle a matter. What this means is that we often turn our questions into statements or declarations, even though we haven't fully embraced understanding. Of course, we understand that the Word of God is not a what, but a who. First off, the Word appears to be a what to the unbeliever and the immature believer, but as we mature in Christ, we should learn to identify the Word as a person. Nevertheless, because we see black letters on a white page, we distance the fonts and the characters printed in our Holy Bibles from the man who laid down His life for us. To us, these are two distinct entities—Jesus is the Son of God, and our Bibles are prophetic words from God designed to help us better understand the heart of God. And while this understanding is elementary in nature, it isn't entirely wrong, but it lacks substance; it lacks depth.

John 1:1-3
In the beginning was the Word, and the Word was with God, and the Word was God. The same was in the beginning with God. All things were made by him; and without him was not anything made that was made. In him was life; and the life was the light of men. And the light shineth in darkness; and the darkness comprehended it not.

To better understand this scripture, we have to understand the word "beginning." This leads us to a couple of scriptures.

Genesis 1:1-2
In the beginning God created the heaven and the earth. And the earth was without form, and void; and darkness *was* upon the face of the deep. And the Spirit of God moved upon the face of the waters.

When we read this scripture, we recognize the word "beginning" as a time, but hear me—this would indicate that God had a starting point. This indicates that there was a period where God did not exist, and then, He came into existence, but we all know that this is not true. YAHWEH has always existed! What this means is that the word "beginning" doesn't mean a space in time, especially since God created time and is therefore not subject to it. Let's look at another scripture to understand this mystery word!

Revelation 22:13
I am the Alpha and the Omega, the Beginning and the End, the First and the Last.

God is the Beginning! This literally means that He is the origin or the starting point for all of creation! What this also means is that Genesis 1:1-2 wasn't referencing a period, it was referencing a location. In other words, when the text says "In the beginning God created the heaven and the earth," it simply means that God created Heaven and the Earth inside of Him! He pulled the raw materials for Heaven and the raw materials for Earth out of Himself! This is why He was able to pull Adam out of the dust and He was able to pull Eve out of Adam! The dust was rich with potential, and that potential manifested itself as mankind. When Adam let out his first breath and opened his eyes, he became a living expression of God's power. He was more than an expression of God's potential, because undeveloped or unexpressed ability is called potential, but once it is expressed, it's called power! When it does what it was created to do, it becomes power-filled or, better yet, powerful. Again, when God references Himself as the Beginning, He's referencing Himself as the Source for all things. Another word for Source is Author.

Hebrews 12:2
Looking unto Jesus the author and finisher of our faith; who for the joy that was set before him endured the cross, despising the shame, and is set down at the right hand of the throne of God.

Hebrews 5:8-10
Though he were a Son, yet learned he obedience by the things which he suffered; and being made perfect, he became the author of eternal salvation unto all them that obey him; called of God an high priest after the order of Melchisedec.

Author	Finisher
Alpha	Omega
Beginning	End

Do you see the correlation? God is the Author of our faith, the Beginning and the Alpha. He is the Finisher, the Omega and the End! What does an author do? An author takes words, brings them together to create a series of expressions, all of which are designed to communicate a message to the readers. The author then publishes that message either via book, magazine, blog post, newspaper, journal or another medium. The goal is to transfer the information from the author's heart to the readers' hearts. This is how the author expresses himself or herself; this is also how the author makes an impartation. So, if God is the Author of our faith and Jesus is the Word of God, how can we best understand the person of Jesus Christ? How can we relate the Word of God to the Man of God? To get a better grasp of this, we must first take a scroll through the scriptures.

Genesis 2:7
And the LORD God formed man of the dust of the ground, and breathed into his nostrils the breath of life; and man became a living soul.

The dust of the ground was tiny particles of what we now refer to as sand, all of which came together to create the first Adam. The dust had potential, but it needed someone to pull out or power up that potential. When God added His breath to Adam, He essentially plugged Adam back into Himself. When Adam sinned against God, YAHWEH then unplugged Himself from mankind. This essentially is what death is. It was God rejecting the dust that man was wrapped in because it had become tainted or dirty. But God wanted to recover His breath! That is the spirit or pneuma of a man, so He sent the Second Adam who, of course, is Jesus Christ. Like the first Adam, God pulled Jesus out of the dust, but this time, the dust was dirty. The dust, of course, was Mary, and when I say dirty, I mean she had a sin nature. Nevertheless, the Father or, better yet, Author of Jesus is, was and will remain perfect. This means that Jesus was half man, but all God. God declared in Isaiah 55:11, “So shall my word be that goeth forth out of my mouth: it shall not return unto me void, but it shall accomplish that which I please, and it shall prosper in the thing whereto I sent it.” Who is Jesus? He is the Word of God, and the scriptures tell us that God is Truth; it is literally impossible for Him to lie. Why is that? Because the minute He speaks a thing, it has to obey; it has to manifest itself, therefore, it is impossible for God to lie. So, when He foretold us in the scriptures about the coming, death and resurrection of Jesus Christ, what He spoke had to materialize!

Isaiah 9:6-7
For unto us a child is born, unto us a son is given: and the government shall be upon his shoulder: and his name shall be called Wonderful, Counseller, The mighty God, The everlasting Father, The Prince of Peace. Of the increase of his government and peace there shall be no end, upon the throne of David, and upon his kingdom, to order it, and to establish

it with judgment and with justice from henceforth even for ever. The zeal of the LORD of hosts will perform this.

This means that Jesus is the Truth. As humans, we understand words because the Word is too complex for our understanding. God had to take Who He is and break Himself down in a way that was palatable to us, so He spoke the Truth and the Truth manifested in the flesh. He is His Word, and the Word is God; the two cannot be separated. If this is too rich for you to understand, just keep studying the scriptures and reread this text until your understanding is opened. The words on the pages of the Bible, however, are the flesh of Jesus.

John 6:54-58
Whoso eateth my flesh, and drinketh my blood, hath eternal life; and I will raise him up at the last day. For my flesh is meat indeed, and my blood is drink indeed. He that eateth my flesh, and drinketh my blood, dwelleth in me, and I in him. As the living Father hath sent me, and I live by the Father: so he that eateth me, even he shall live by me. This is that bread which came down from heaven: not as your fathers did eat manna, and are dead: he that eateth of this bread shall live for ever.

Luke 22:19
And he took bread, and gave thanks, and brake it, and gave unto them, saying, This is my body which is given for you: this do in remembrance of me.

When Jesus said that we are to eat His flesh, He wasn't literally talking about the earth suit He was wrapped in, He was talking about the scriptures! Jesus' body was taken up to Heaven, so we couldn't literally eat His flesh. The flesh of Jesus is the Logos, Graphe and Rhema of God! Our job is to take the Word and ingest Him (not it) until we look, walk, smell and talk like Him! This means that the Word of God is the expression of God revealed.

Internalized	**Materialized**
Potential	**Power**

Jesus is the living Word of God; He is the Truth, the Way and the Life. He is God Himself because God is not separate from His Word!

The Words of God

Now, that we understand who the Word of God is, it's important for us to understand the words of God. These are the black and white letters carefully printed on the pages of our Bibles. To understand this, I want you to look at the alphabets below.

A	B	C	D	E	F	G	H	I	J	K	L	M
N	O	P	Q	R	S	T	U	V	W	X	Y	Z

The alphabets are for humans, of course. To form a word, I couldn't just grab any random series of alphabets, I'd have to carefully select the letters that make up already established words. If I put together, for example, “qtijabromznp,” you wouldn't understand what I was saying because it's not an actual word. It's a bunch of letters carelessly thrown together for no other reason than to prove a point. But if I put together, “quiet,” you would understand this word to mean “be silent.” The word “silent” is a synonym of the word “quiet.” All the same, Jesus is a synonym of God!

To make Jesus more palatable to the human, God had to create a method that would allow Him to communicate with man since man no longer understood spiritual things. The Semitic people are credited for creating the alphabets; these people were polytheistic, meaning, they worshiped many gods. So, why then would God use them to create the alphabets? Romans 11:29 answers this question for us.

Romans 11:29
For the gifts and calling of God are without repentance.

Remember, God created Adam from His own potential, and when Adam was made, God's potential manifested His power. Every human being on the face of this planet, whether saved or unsaved, came from the first Adam. This means that every human has good in him or her, but when sin entered into man, it became another belly of potential that man could draw from. What this essentially means is that regardless of whether we believe God or not, we still have His nature underneath the dirt that is our flesh. And we can express this potential regardless of whether we are saved or not. There are some expressions, however, that are reserved for believers, of course. Think about every granule of dirt that it took to make up Adam's body; these individual granules are the equivalent of letters. God didn't just grab a bunch of sand and create Adam. He carefully selected each granule that would make up his body. This was the equivalent of Him taking a bunch of letters and forming words. Once those words came together, they were pretty much like an unpublished book. When God breathed life into Adam, He essentially published him. He then equipped Adam with the blessing and the curse of "will." This is the ability to make a conscious choice. In other words, the Author and Finisher of our faith handed the pen of Adam's life to him and allowed him to write his own story. Somehow, along the way, Adam added a twist to his story that caused it to no longer be a good story, but it became a polluted or perverted piece of work. Sin caused Adam to break back down into individual letters or granules of dirt called atoms. Jesus came along and swept up these letters, but He didn't reform them. Instead, He stood in our place! He became the words, while we became the Word! Nevertheless, because there was no sin in Him, death couldn't keep Him, and hell had to loose Him! Nowadays, the words of God is the body of Jesus broken down in such a way that allows us to ingest Him until we manifest ourselves as the Word or, better yet, the living expression of God's heart and will in the Earth! To be made whole means to sweep up or clean up our acts through the study and application of the Word; that is, until our lives make sense to us and everyone who sees us! When He took the bread and broke it for His disciples at the last supper, He was metaphorically breaking Himself down in a way that would allow us to receive Him.

So, who are the words of God? We are, but we still have to take the Word of God and ingest Him until we manifest as the very image of God! Who is the Word of God? Jesus Christ is still the Word of God. He never abdicated His throne; He simply exchanged places with us so that we too could be seated in heavenly places!

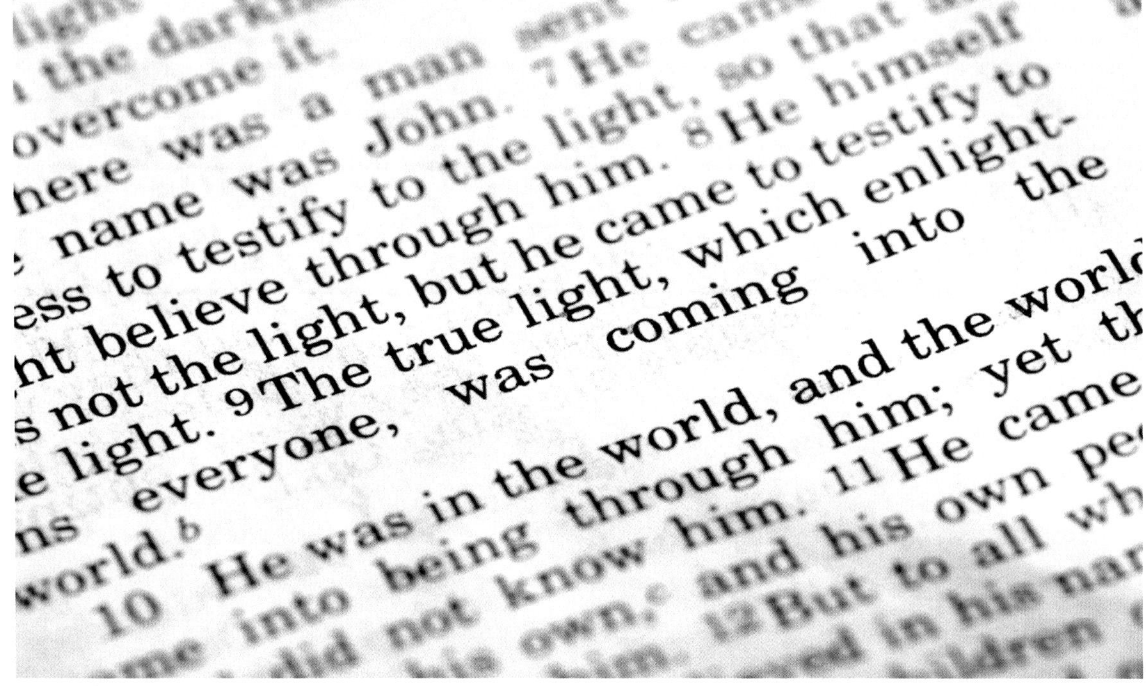

12 Historical Bible Facts

#1

The word "Bible" comes from the Greek word "ta biblia," which literally means "the scrolls" or "the books." The word "Bible" originates from the ancient city of Byblos, which was located in Lebanon. Byblos used to be the official supplier of paper products to the ancient world.

#2

John Wycliffe produced the first translation of the entire Bible from Latin Vulgate into English. After he died, the Catholic Church exhumed his body and burned his corpse. This was a punishment for his translation work.

#3

William Tyndale produced the first printed and edited version of the New Testament in English. Church authorities in England tried to prevent him from translating the Bible so he went to Germany and translated it. He was later convicted of heresy and executed by strangulation. His body was burned at the stake for his efforts.

#4

The word "bible" comes from the Greek word "ta biblia," which literally means "the scrolls" or "the books." The word "bible" originates from the ancient city of Byblos, which was located in Lebanon. Byblos used to be the official supplier of paper products to the ancient world.

#5

The King James Bible contains:
788,258 words
31,102 verses
1,189 chapters
66 books

#6

The world's largest Bible was built by Louis Waynai in 1930.
It has 8,048 pages and weighs 1,094 pounds.
This Bible is 43.5 inches tall.

#7

The Bible we use today is called the Protestant Bible, and it contains 66 books, with 39 of those books being the Old Testament and 27 of those books being the New Testament.

#8

The Bible was written well over 1400 years ago, with the Old Testament written between 1200 and 165 BC and the New Testament written between 50 and 100 AD.

#9

The New Testament is divided up into two parts; they are the Gospels (Matthew, Mark, Luke and John) and the Letters (epistles).

#10

The Old Testament was originally written in Hebrew, but the New Testament was mainly written in Greek.

#11

The first five Books of the Bible (Genesis, Exodus, Leviticus, Numbers, Deuteronomy) are called the Pentateuch. They are also called "the Law." The Hebrew word for "law" is Torah.

#12

The Prophets is the largest section of the Hebrew Bible, and has two parts, which are "former prophets" and "latter prophets."

YAHWEH (THE TRUE AND LIVING GOD)

Who is God? Most of us have embraced a fundamental, elementary idea of who He is, rather than getting to know Him intimately. The reason behind this logic is because relationships take a LOT of work to build! And what I've come to learn is that the average American does NOT know the basics of building strong, healthy, life-long relationships. This is partly due to the many "isms" that divide our society, and these dividing lines don't just separate races, they separate believers. This is because our culture has taught us to "get in where we fit in." Using this logic, what we've learned to do is surround ourselves with people who are on or beneath our levels mentally, spiritually and/or socially. This allows us the luxury of not having someone who has a perspective contrary to or higher than our own to stretch, challenge and reason with us. In other words, we are terrified of what's on the other side of our prisons of comfort, and we've carried this fear into our relationship with God. Consequently, we get to know the basics of who God is, some of what He's done, and the a, b, c's of what He stands for. And hear me—willful ignorance is as costly as the crime of rebellion!

If I were to ask you to give me ten of God's names, would you be able to do so without searching this book or searching the scriptures? If I were to ask you to share with me ten characteristics that describe God, would you be able to do so? If not, don't feel bad; you're in good company. Again, we haven't been encouraged to get to know God; instead, we've been locked up behind the four walls of our churches, treating scriptures like catchphrases and dancing around our dysfunctions. The great news is, we can be uninformed today, but be in a far better place tomorrow! This is why I compiled a list of God's names, titles and scriptures designed to help us get to know Him on a more intimate spectrum! Study His names every day. At least, memorize two of His names and titles a day, and incorporate them into your prayer life.

WHEN JESUS CAME INTO THE COASTS OF CAESAREA PHILIPPI, HE ASKED HIS DISCIPLES, SAYING, WHOM DO MEN SAY THAT I THE SON OF MAN AM?

The Names of God

Name	Meaning
ABIR	Mighty One
ADONAI	Master or Lord
BRANCH	Extension of God
EL	The Strong One
EL BERITH	God of the Covenant
EL ELYON	Most High
EL GIBHOR	Mighty God
EL OLAM	Everlasting God
EL ROI	God of Seeing
ELOHIM	God
EL SHADDAI	God Almighty or "God All Sufficient"
EMMANUEL	God With Us
EYALUTH	Strength
FATHER	2 Samuel
GAOL	Redeemer
JEHOVAH	LORD (YAHWEH)
JEHOVAH ELOHIM	LORD God
JEHOVAH JIREH	The Lord Will Provide
JEHOVAH MEKODDISHKEM	The Lord Who Sanctifies
JEHOVAH-NISSI	The Lord Our Banner
JEHOVAH RAAH	The Lord My Shepherd
JEHOVAH-RAPHA	The Lord Who Heals
JEHOVAH-ROHI	The Lord Our Shepherd
JEHOVAH-SABAOTH	The Lord of Hosts
JEHOVAH-SHALOM	The Lord Our Peace

Name	Meaning
JEHOVAH-SHAMMAH	The Lord is There
JEHOVAH-TSIDKENU	The Lord Our Righteousness
KADOSH	Holy One
KANNA	Jealous God
MAGEN	Shield
MELEKH	King
PALET	Deliverer
SHAPHAT	Judge
SHEPHERD	Pastor
TSADDIQ	Righteous One
TSUR	God our Rock
YAHWEH	Lord, JEHOVAH
YESHUA	Savior

Other Names and/or Titles of God

Please note that while this is an exhaustive list, it is not a complete one.

Name/Title	Scripture	Name/Title	Scripture
Abba	Romans 8:15	**Light of the World**	John 8:12; John 9:5
Advocate	1 John 2:1	**Lion of the Tribe of Judah**	Revelation 5:5
Almighty	Revelation 1:8	**Living Water**	John 4:10
Alpha	Revelation 1:8	**Lord**	Deuteronomy 10:17
Amen	Revelation 3:14	**Lord of Hosts**	Isaiah 47:4
Anchor of the Soul	Hebrews 6:19	**Man of War**	Exodus 15:3
Ancient of Days	Daniel 7:9	**Master**	Matthew 23:8
Angel of the Lord	Genesis 16:7	**Mediator**	1 Timothy 2:5

Name/Title	Scripture	Name/Title	Scripture
Anointed One	Psalm 2:2	**Messiah**	John 1:41
Apostle	Hebrews 3:1	**Mighty God**	Isaiah 9:6
Architect	Hebrews 11:10	**Mighty Warrior**	Jeremiah 20:11
Author and Perfecter of our Faith	Hebrews 12:2	**Morning Star**	Revelation 22:16
Beginning	Revelation 21:6	**Most High God**	
Bishop of Souls	1 Peter 2:25	**Nazarene**	Matthew 2:23
Branch	Zechariah 3:8	**Omega**	Revelation 1:8
Bread of Life	John 6:35,48	**Passover Lamb**	1 Corinthians 5:7
Bridegroom	Matthew 9:15	**Physician**	Matthew 9:12
Builder	1 Corinthians 3:10	**Potentate**	1 Timothy 6:15
Builder of Jerusalem	Psalm 147:2	**Potter**	Isaiah 64:8
Carpenter	Mark 6:3	**Pride of Jacob**	Amos 8:7
Captain of the Host	Joshua 5:14	**Priest**	Hebrews 4:15
Chief Cornerstone	Ephesians 2:20	**Prince**	Acts 5:31
Chief Shepherd	1 Peter 5:4	**Prince of Life**	Acts 3:15
Christ	Matthew 1:16	**Prince of Peace**	Isaiah 9:6
Comforter	Jeremiah 8:18	**Prophet**	Acts 3:22
Consolation of Israel	Luke 2:25	**Propitiation**	I John 2:2
Consuming Fire	Hebrews 12:29	**Purifier**	Malachi 3:3
Dayspring	Luke 1:78	**Rabbi**	John 1:49
Day Star	2 Peter 1:19	**Ransom**	1 Timothy 2:6
Defender	Proverbs 23:11	**Redeemer**	Isaiah 41:14
Deliverer	Romans 11:26	**Refiner**	Malachi 3:2
Desire of All Nations	Haggai 2:7	**Refuge**	Isaiah 25:4
Emmanuel	Matthew 1:23	**Resurrection**	John 11:25
End	Revelation 21:6	**Righteous One**	Proverbs 21:12
Everlasting Father	Isaiah 9:6	**Righteous Judge**	2 Timothy 4:8

Name/Title	Scripture	Name/Title	Scripture
Faithful and True Witness	Revelation 3:14	**Righteousness**	Jeremiah 23:6
Father of Glory	Ephesians 1:17	**Rock**	Deuteronomy 32:4
First Fruits	1 Corinthians 15:23	**Root of David**	Revelation 22:16
Fortress	2 Samuel 22:2	**Rose of Sharon**	Song of Solomon 2:1
Foundation	Isaiah 28:16	**Ruler of All Things**	Colossians 1:16
Fountain	Zechariah 13:1	**Ruler of God's Creation**	Revelation 3:14
Friend of Sinners	Matthew 11:19	**Sacrifice**	Ephesians 5:2
Gate for the Sheep	John 10:7	**Savior**	Luke 1:47
Gift of God	2 Corinthians 9:15	**Savior of All Men**	1 Timothy 4:10
God	John 1:1	**Second Adam**	1 Corinthians 15:47
God of Gods	Deuteronomy 10:17	**Seed of Abraham**	Galatians 3:16
Glory of God	Isaiah 60:1	**Seed of David**	2 Timothy 2:8
Glory of Israel	1 Samuel 15:29	**Seed of the Woman**	Genesis 3:15
Good Shepherd	John 10:11	**Servant**	Isaiah 42:1
Governor	Matthew 2:6	**Shelter**	Psalm 91:2
Great Shepherd	Hebrews 13:20	**Shepherd**	1 Peter 2:25
Guide	Psalm 48:14	**Shield**	Proverbs 30:5
Head of the Church	Colossians 1:18	**Shiloh**	Genesis 49:10
High Priest	Hebrews 3:1	**Son of David**	Matthew 15:22
Holy	Psalm 99:3	**Son of God**	Luke 1:35
Holy One of Israel	Isaiah 41:14	**Son of Man**	Matthew 18:11
Home of Justice	Jeremiah 31:23	**Son of Mary**	Mark 6:3
Hope of Israel	Jeremiah 14:8	**Son of the Most High**	Luke 1:32
Horn of Salvation	Luke 1:69	**Stone**	Isaiah 28:16
I Am	Exodus 3:14	**Strength of Israel**	1 Samuel 15:29

Name/Title	Scripture	Name/Title	Scripture
Image of the Invisible God	Colossians 1:15	**Strong Deliverer**	Psalm 140:7
Jehovah	Psalm 83:18	**Strong Tower**	Psalm 61:3
Jesus	Matthew 1:21	**Sun of Righteousness**	Malachi 4:2
King of Glory	Psalm 24:8	**Teacher**	Matthew 26:18
King of Israel	Matthew 27:42	**Truth**	John 14:6
King of Kings	1 Timothy 6:15	**Vine**	John 15:1
Lamb of God	John 1:29	**Way**	John 14:6
Last Adam	1 Corinthians 15:45	**Wonderful Counselor**	Isaiah 9:6
Life	John 11:25	**Word**	John 1:1
Light of Israel	Isaiah 10:17	**Word of God**	Revelation 19:13

Challenge #1

List ten names of God that you've seen manifesting in your life this week alone!

Challenge #2

This challenge will help to increase you in the area of prayer!

Write and publish a prayer on social media using some of the names of God that you listed in Challenge #1. Detail what God has done for you, and why you're referencing each of the names you've chosen.

Your Prayer

YAHWEH

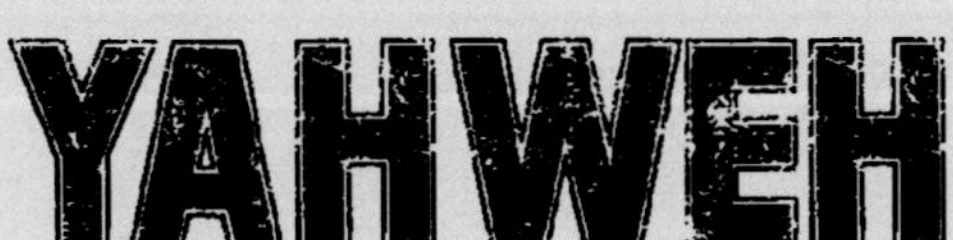

THE NAMES OF GOD

```
F R R H R K T F G E H J K Y R N L F N
N M N A Z G D N T W L X M V K K L G J
L T E M Q M X L A W K E P Z J I R E H
X Y L M X H L K N Y R C L Y H F N N L
N M G A T A M K N M E R P Y Q K I L Z
B M I H X A N E A Q X S N T O Z S K H
X Q B S Z R R U K F E C H D Y N S L A
N D H B L N N L L O S L G U T M I T V
H V O M N K M K E W D A S C A N Q J O
J T R G E A M R J F J D B H I K R C H
G G D D L A K Z R Q M M I A A W M L E
L V I O H M R C B I B X N S O D H H J
N S L P W H K F Y L L O J B H T D X G
T E A E A Q C A S G D Y N H B K H A K
Z R M L B C H L H A Q C Y A H W E H I
T V N O B C G Z A J N E L R O I L M T
G P M H A Y T N L Q F G E L E L O A H
D T L I J Z N F O R O H I H H P G K N
M Z V M Y W T H M X H M R K J B W G C
```

Abba
Adonai
Chayim
El Eloah
El Elyon
El Gibhor
El Kanna
Elohim
El Olam
El Roi
El Shaddai
Jehovah
Jireh
Mekoddishkem
Nissi
Raah
Rapha
Rohi
Sabaoth
Shalom
Shammah
Tsideknu
Yahweh
Yeshua

The Great I AM

Exodus 3:14
And God said unto Moses, I AM THAT I AM: and he said, Thus shalt thou say unto the children of Israel, I AM hath sent me unto you.

John 6:35
And Jesus said unto them, I am the bread of life: he that cometh to me shall never hunger; and he that believeth on me shall never thirst.

John 6:48
I am that bread of life.

John 8:12
Then spake Jesus again unto them, saying, I am the light of the world: he that followeth me shall not walk in darkness, but shall have the light of life.

John 8:58
Jesus said unto them, Verily, verily, I say unto you, Before Abraham was, I am.

John 9:5
As long as I am in the world, I am the light of the world.

John 10:9
I am the door: by me if any man enter in, he shall be saved, and shall go in and out, and find pasture.

John 10:11
I am the good shepherd: the good shepherd giveth his life for the sheep.

John 10:14
I am the good shepherd, and know my sheep, and am known of mine.

John 11:25
Jesus said unto her, I am the resurrection, and the life: he that believeth in me, though he were dead, yet shall he live.

John 14:6
Jesus saith unto him, I am the way, the truth, and the life: no man cometh unto the Father, but by me.

John 15:1
I am the true vine, and my Father is the husbandman.

John 15:5
I am the vine, ye *are* the branches: He that abideth in me, and I in him, the same bringeth forth much fruit: for without me ye can do nothing.

Revelation 1:8
I am Alpha and Omega, the beginning and the ending, saith the Lord, which is, and which was, and which is to come, the Almighty.

The Effects of Biblical Ignorance

A woman flies to Egypt, and while there, she purchases her a large bottle of Nair Hair Removal Creme. Unbeknownst to her, what she's purchasing is designed to remove hair from the legs and the armpits, but she wants to perm the hair on her head. Because she can't read the words on the bottle, she assumes that the crème inside the bottle is designed to straighten her hair like the kits she's used back home to straighten her hair. This is because Nair smells identical to the traditional perm used by women with curly or coarse hair. Not wanting to look ignorant or wrestle through the language barrier by asking questions, she decides to purchase the Nair, along with a bottle of shampoo and a bottle of conditioner. Later that day, she arrives in her hotel room, excited about her plans for the following day. She removes the rubber band from her long silky ponytail, divides her hair into four sections and then proceeds to apply the Nair to her hair. We all know how this story ends. She lost most of her hair and her trip was ruined. But wait! She was ignorant of what she was putting on her hair! Shouldn't she then be exempt from the effects of the hair removal crème? No! It did what it was designed to do. Hear me—ignorance is an excuse, not an exemption! What you don't know can hurt you, regardless of how unfair you think it is! Think about it this way—a two-year old stands on a live ant pile, completely ignorant of the dangers beneath his feet. Seconds later, he begins to scream, run around and frantically dust his legs and feet with his hands. He tosses his little body to the ground and begins to roll and scratch his legs. His mother rushes over and removes the rest of the ants from his legs and rushes him into the house so that she can bathe him and treat his injuries. But wait! He's just a toddler! Why didn't the ants take his age into consideration before attacking him? It's simple. They are not human, nor do they submit to human logic! The point is, ignorance is one of the most expensive crimes underneath the sun, and many have paid the ultimate price for it! Just like that toddler, being a babe in Christ won't exempt us from the laws that govern nature and spirituality. Ignorance can never serve as an exemption.

One of the greatest dangers surrounding ignorance is that you'll repeatedly put yourself in harm's way. An animal lover who's never read a book, watched television, scrolled the internet or traveled outside of, for example, Europe, may not know that a lion is a dangerous creature. If she were to travel to Africa, go on a safari and see a lion, her ignorance could cause her to unknowingly volunteer to be a lion's first meal of the day. The lion doesn't care about her history with animals or her good intentions. Her ignorance just made its job a lot easier! The same is true for Satan! He doesn't care if you are biblically illiterate! He won't pass you by just because your phone has more of your fingerprints on it than your Bible!

First and foremost, let's define the word "ignorant," since it is where we get the word "ignorance," which means the state of being ignorant. Ignorance, as defined by Merriam Webster is:

1. destitute of knowledge or education
2. lacking knowledge or comprehension of the thing specified
3. resulting from or showing lack of knowledge or intelligence
4. uninformed, unaware

For centuries on end, man has used ignorance as an excuse for his laziness, his procrastination and his rebellion. And for centuries on end, man has had to manage the penalties associated with not digging. Genesis 2:15 reads, "And the LORD God took the man, and put him into the garden of Eden to dress it and to keep it." God took Adam from the dust, and then He gave Adam the responsibility of cultivating the dust. This is so the earth could spring forth its potential. But get this—Adam was the earth or the very dust he was charged to turn, to water and to cultivate! In other words, Adam's assignment was designed to get him to understand who he was and what was in him! But if he didn't dig, he wouldn't see the earth's potential; if he didn't turn the ground, he would have never known what was underneath it! In Genesis 3:17-19, Adam is being arraigned for rebelling against God.

Genesis 3:17-19
And unto Adam he said, Because thou hast hearkened unto the voice of thy wife, and hast eaten of the tree, of which I commanded thee, saying, Thou shalt not eat of it: cursed is the ground for thy sake; in sorrow shalt thou eat of it all the days of thy life; thorns also and thistles shall it bring forth to thee; and thou shalt eat the herb of the field; in the sweat of thy face shalt thou eat bread, till thou return unto the ground; for out of it wast thou taken: for dust thou art, and unto dust shalt thou return.

Because there was no sin in the ground, Adam's assignment was initially a sweatless victory. In other words, it didn't require too much effort; it didn't require pain and it didn't require him to tire himself out. He didn't have to cut away at weeds, prick his fingers on thorns or pull parasites off of what he had been entrusted to grow. All he had to do was pull out the earth's potential, and by doing so, he would simultaneously pull out his own potential. But after sin got into the dust, the dust became contaminated (dirty); in other words, Adam not only had to discipline his flesh, he now had thorns (perversions) and thistles (strongholds) that he had to pull down, chop down and cast down in order for the earth (and himself) to yield its potential. The Apostle Paul talked about this wrestling match in 2 Corinthians 12:17, when he was dealing with his own perversions. It reads, "And lest I should be exalted above measure through the abundance of the revelations, there was given to me a <u>thorn in the flesh</u>, the messenger of Satan to buffet me, lest I should be exalted above measure."

Thorns (Flesh)	Thistles (Mind)
Perversions	Strongholds

Again, to be ignorant simply means to be unaware or uninformed, but get this—lack of awareness doesn't always equate to innocence! Sometimes, choosing not to know something is still considered rebellion. Consider this situation. A young man tells his mother that he's about to go out with his ex-girlfriend. According to him, they're just going to talk about the failure of their relationship so that they can both get some closure. The mother knows that the ex-girlfriend doesn't need closure. She's already moved on, but her son has been crying, complaining and calling the girl for weeks on end to discuss the events that led up to their breakup. And finally, the young lady agrees to meet with him, hoping that they can part ways on good terms. Nevertheless, the night takes a dark turn, and the young man returns home wearing a blood-stained t-shirt and he has a few scratches on his face. When he opens the door, the mother walks into the living room and notices the blood, the scratches and all of the dirt, leaves and debris covering her son. He's crying and disoriented, but in that moment, his mother makes a decision. He opens his mouth to tell her what happened, but she quickly silences him by placing her index finger in front of her lips. She then shakes her head and stretches out her hand, silently indicating that she wants her son to remove the clothes he's wearing and hand them to her. Realizing what his mother wants, he pulls off his shirt and hands it to her. She tosses it into a bag while he takes off his pants. “Mom, I just wanted to talk,” he says, but once again, his mother silences him. “I don't want to hear about it. Just go and take a shower. I'll deal with the rest.” A few weeks later, her son is arrested for first degree murder and the mother is arrested for obstruction of justice for tampering with evidence and failure to report a crime. Her defense? “I didn't know. He didn't tell me anything!” Does this mean that her ignorance keeps her from being found guilty? No! She was willfully ignorant, just like many people in the body of Christ. Ignorance does not equate to innocence! An ignorant man playing with fire would get the same degree of burns as a firefighter playing with that same fire!

Biblical illiteracy has become a MAJOR issue in the body of Christ, especially amongst Millennials and Generation Z. Consequently, we see a lot of believers who do not and will not follow biblical protocol, believers who use their ignorance as a license to rebel against God and leadership. Additionally, we eventually see the effects of their rebellion ripping through their flesh, their finances and their minds! This is because rebellion is a thistle; it's a stronghold of the mind that expresses itself through the flesh, and just like any thistle, once it drops a series of seeds, it swiftly begins to dominate a garden until that garden becomes unusable. Northern Dakota State University reported the following, “Most thistles in the western United States are native species that generally go unnoticed and likely never will cause significant losses as weeds. However, thistle species introduced from Europe, Africa and Asia can be very aggressive opportunists. They often invade overused or otherwise disturbed land. The plants spread rapidly and out-compete established and introduced plant species for nutrients, and can render pastures, rangeland and forests nearly unusable" (Source: Northern Dakota State University/Perennial and Biennial Thistle Control/W-799/Rod Lym, Professor, Plant Sciences). A few facts about thistles include:

1. They are wild; they are weeds. Another word for weed is a wildflower, meaning, a flower or plant that is not planted or welcomed in a garden, but is instead blown there by the wind. In other words, they have no order or structure.
2. Many weeds overproduce seeds, eventually dominating the garden, thus discouraging the planted flowers or fruits from producing so that the weeds can continue producing. In other words, they steal the ground that was reserved by the farmer or gardener for whatever it is that he or she had been planting.
3. Weeds compete for sunlight, nutrients and water that would have otherwise served as food for the plants of that garden. This causes the planted flowers and fruits to die, while the weeds take over the garden.

Again, rebellion is a thistle, and it continues to spread until the believer has ruined or caused damage to every organization or structure he or she was once a part of. Eventually, it begins to consume the believer himself or herself; this is especially true when the believer has damaged a lot of structures, thus, causing most people to not trust that particular believer. This is when the believer loses ground, and the stronghold starts to consume his or her mind. We've seen this before, but for the most part, we've been too afraid to point it out! We've seen, for example, men and women coming up against the church at large, attempting to expose pastors and encouraging rebellion amongst believers. We've witnessed the damage they've done, the platforms they've built on top of the graves of whatever it is they've destroyed, and we've watched them crumble right before our very eyes! We've seen them go back into the world, dabble with drugs and descend deeper and deeper into madness! This is because unchecked thistles can and do rapidly colonize; they can cover or spread between six to twelve miles in a single year! And what's worse is animals that graze will not eat them because they are covered with pricks! So, they're left to grow and dominate a garden until it becomes a field.

Other effects of biblical ignorance or illiteracy include, but are not limited to:

1. **Believers who are biblically illiterate are unaware of their identities:** Your identity is directly connected to your inheritance, your authenticity and your calling.
2. **Believers who are biblically ignorant are unaware of their authority:** Consequently, these believers tolerate and sometimes even partner with demons that they have the authority to cast down and cast out!

3. **Believers who are biblically illiterate typically find themselves in cycles!** This is the very nature of a stronghold! In other words, they keep doing the same thing, hoping to get a different result. This is the very definition of insanity!
4. **Believers who are biblically ignorant diminish the quality of their lives.** We were created to look and think like God! But when we deny ourselves this opportunity because we refuse to study the heart and character of God, we spend our lives looking like what we've been through.
5. **Believers who are biblically ignorant can and do shorten their lifespans!** In Hosea 4:6, God said, "My people are destroyed for lack of knowledge."
6. **Believers who are biblically ignorant lose ground!** This is because they don't know or understand their authority! What does it mean to lose ground? Think about the gardener or the farmer. He plants a field, but finds that the field has been invaded by thorns and thistles. If he doesn't know where his garden starts and ends, he will continue to lose ground one inch at a time! When a believer loses ground, that believer loses more and more of the real estate in his or her mind. When the enemy has stolen enough of the believer's mental real estate, believers start becoming more and more mystical and paranoid.
7. **Believers who are biblically illiterate are the starting points or continuations of generational strongholds!** Generational curses are nothing but strongholds of the mind (thistles) and perversions (thorns) that continue to spread generation after generation until it consumes and/or eradicates a bloodline! This is why you'll see some families where, for example, sexual perversion has taken completely over the family, and just about every family member wrestles with some form of sexual deviancy.

Biblical ignorance or illiteracy is the reason this world is in the state of shambles it's in today. Most believers do not know their authority because they have not embraced their identities. Consequently, we see an increase in crimes and sin, and we will continue to see this until the church (the individual granules or, better yet, people who make up the church) collectively and individually begin to open their Bibles, bend their knees and pursue the intimate knowledge of God!

"FACTS DO NOT CEASE TO EXIST BECAUSE THEY ARE IGNORED."

Aldous Huxley, Complete Essays 2, 1926-29

Numbers in the Bible

Numbers in the biblical text are important because they help us to understand the patterns or the rhythms of God. Think of it this way. Chances are, you know the patterns or habits of the people closest to you. How did you get to know their idiosyncrasies? Through relationship, of course! You've learned their personalized customs, routines and quirks through intimacy. And hear me—intimacy isn't a sexual term; it literally means closeness. The closer you are to someone, the more you are affected by that person's decisions. Here's another way to look at it—if you were walking shoulder-to-shoulder with someone, every time that person moved, you'd feel his or her movement. This is because you are in one another's intimate space! But if there was at least a foot of space between the two of you, you would not feel that person's movements. The further that person is from you physically, the less aware you will be of that person. Intimacy is mental closeness! You can't get close to God by chanting scriptures or performing a bunch of religious calisthenics! To get close to Him, you have to pursue Him, and you do this by studying His movements! In other words, you become an avid student of, not just the scriptures, but the living Word of God, meaning, they aren't just words on a paper to you. The scriptures have to become a person; they have to become Jesus Christ standing right in front of you! This is your daily bread; this is your personal encounter with Him! To get close to God, you have to syncopate your movements with His! And one of the ways to do this is learn the many ways in which He communicates with us, including through numerical patterns.

Let's look at some popular numbers in the scriptures to get a better understanding of what they represent!

1	2	3	4	5

Number One

1

This is the only number in the world that is completely independent of any and every other numeral! The number one can only be divided by itself, and even then, it still reproduces itself.

1	Divided by	1	Equals	1
Father		Son		Holy Spirit

Therefore, the number one is significant of the God head. It represents the indivisible nature of God.

Number Two

2

The number two deals with the coming together of two people or, better yet, a union. Nevertheless, each unit in a union has the sole responsibility of honoring the Word of God so that the two can be one person! This isn't just true for marriage, but it also deals with Christ coming together with the church. Notice that throughout the scriptures, a marriage could only be divided by two or more witnesses. This is because two divided by two equals one. All the same, God told Adam and Eve to be fruitful and MULTIPLY! Nevertheless, in spiritual multiplication, two times two equals one.

Number Three

3

The number three represents completeness or wholeness. Christ was dead for three days before He was resurrected. The Magi presented three gifts to Jesus: gold, frankincense, and myrrh in Matthew 2. Of course, we know that God is three in one.

Father	Son	Holy Spirit

Number Four

4

The number four deals with creation. There are four gospel accounts of Jesus' life and ministry. God completed the framework for the universe on day four. On the fourth day, He created the sun, the moon and the stars. Of course, there are four seasons in a year (Spring, Summer, Fall, Winter). There are four gospels, of course.

Matthew	Mark	Luke	John

Number Five

5

Five is the number of grace! Of course, the Ten Commandments were broken up into two tablets, with five commandments on each (double grace). There were five offering types that God told Israel to bring Him.

Burnt Offering	Sin Offering	Trespass Offering	Grain Offering	Peace Offering

There are five books of God's Law.

Genesis	Exodus	Leviticus	Numbers	Deuteronomy

And of course, there is the five-fold ministry officers.

Apostle	Prophet	Evangelist	Teacher	Pastor

Of course, the number six means human fallibility and flesh. Man was created on the sixth day. It is also a number that represents the evils of Satan. The number seven is the number of perfection! The number twelve is the number of government; it represents power and authority! Again, if you study the patterns of God in the scriptures, you'll learn more of how He uses numbers to communicate with us.

Seven Dispensations of the Bible

In Christian theology, there are seven dispensations of the Bible. According to theopedia.com, dispensationalism is, "a theological system that teaches biblical history is best understood in light of a number of successive administrations of God's dealings with mankind, which it calls 'dispensations.' It maintains fundamental distinctions between God's plans for national Israel and for the New Testament Church, and emphasizes prophecy of the end-times and a pre-tribulation rapture of the church prior to Christ's Second Coming."

Innocence

This is the time prior to Adam's fall, when man was sinless. This is the period when Adam and Eve lived in the Garden of Eden. During this period, God walked freely with mankind. Adam and Eve were given the following commandments:

1	Be fruitful
2	Multiply
3	Replenish the earth
4	Subdue the Earth
5	Have dominion over the fish of the sea, the fowl of the air, and over every living thing that moveth upon the earth.
6	To not touch or eat from the Tree of the Knowledge of Good and Evil.

This dispensation ended when man rebelled against God and was evicted from the Garden of Eden.

Conscience

The period between the fall and the Great Flood. This dispensation lasted 1,656 years. This is when God allowed man's conscience to govern his decisions. Consequently, man grew more and more wicked, so God decided to destroy the Earth with a flood.

Human Government

Beginning in Genesis 8, this is the period immediately after the Great Flood when God used Noah to reestablish or restart the human race. During this dispensation, God made the following promises to Noah:

God will not curse the earth again.
Noah and family are to replenish the earth with people.
They shall have dominion over the animal creation.
They are allowed to eat meat.
The law of capital punishment is established.
There never will be another worldwide flood.
The sign of God’s promise will be the rainbow.

Promise

This describes the period from Abraham to Moses. Also known as the period of the Abrahamic Law, this dispensation started with the calling of Abram. Noah's family hadn't filled the Earth like God commanded them to; instead, all of mankind walked about as one big group. This is when the Tower of Babel was built, causing God to confuse the language of the people and scatter them about the Earth. During this dispensation, God made a promise to Abram that He would multiply his seeds and make him the father of many nations. This dispensation ended with the deliverance of God's people from captivity in Egypt.

Law

Period from Moses to the crucifixion of Jesus. Also referred to as Mosaic Law, this is the period in which the Ten Commandments were birthed. This dispensation lasted 1,500 years from Exodus until the crucifixion of Jesus.

Grace Period

This is the period from the cross to the rapture of the church. This is where we currently are. This dispensation began with the New Covenant established by the blood of Jesus and will end with the rapture of the church. Because of Jesus's sacrifice, we are no longer under the Law of works, but are instead governed by grace.

Millennial Kingdom

The period when Jesus reigns on Earth for one thousand years, followed by another rebellion, and will end with God's judgment.

Challenge Yourself

Using the calendar below, list every significant event that has taken place for you this week, and list every significant event that takes place over the next four weeks. The reason this is important is because the end and start of every given season is marked by an event. We call this a shift. Knowing when this shift occurs will help us to identify the end/start of a season.

Sunday	Monday	Tuesday	Wednesday	Thursday	Friday	Saturday

Seven Mountains of Influence

Established in 1975 by Bill Bright (founder of Campus Crusade) and Loren Cunningham (founder of Youth with a Mission), the Seven Mountain Mandate, also known as dominion theology, was a dream given to the two men (unbeknownst to one another). Mr. Bright and Mr. Cunningham had lunch together, where they shared the prophetic dream they'd had with one another. Another man by the name of Francis Schaeffer had received a similar message from the Lord.

In short, the Seven Mountain Mandate dictates that Christians are to rule over the Seven Societal Mountains of Influence, which are:

Mountain of Religion
Mountain of Family
Mountain of Education
Mountain of Government
Mountain of Arts and Entertainment
Mountain of Media
Mountain of Business

Of course, like any prophetic message, the Seven Mountain Mandate has received a lot of criticism, and has even been called heretic. Nevertheless, the book of Revelations actually confirms this prophecy when he describes the seven-headed beast, which we know to be Satan. Satan has been ruling over these mountains, and it is the job of the Christian to carry out the instructions that God gave Adam in the Garden of Eden, which includes:

1. Subdue the Earth
2. Have dominion over the fish of the sea, the fowl of the air, and over every living thing that moveth upon the earth.

Revelation 13:1
And I stood upon the sand of the sea, and saw a beast rise up out of the sea, having seven heads and ten horns, and upon his horns ten crowns, and upon his heads the name of blasphemy.

Five Covenants in the Bible

The Noahic Covenant
Genesis 9:11
I establish my covenant with you, that never again shall all flesh be cut off by the waters of the flood, and never again shall there be a flood to destroy the earth.

The Abrahamic Covenant
Genesis 12:1-3
Now the Lord had said to Abram: 'Get out of your country, from your family and from your father's house, to a land that I will show you. I will make you a great nation; I will bless you and make your name great; and you shall be a blessing. I will bless those who bless you, and I will curse him who curses you; and in you all the families of the earth shall be blessed.

The Mosaic Covenant
Genesis 12:1-3
Now therefore, if you will indeed obey My voice and keep My covenant, then you shall be a special treasure to Me above all people; for all the earth is Mine. And you shall be to Me a kingdom of priests and a holy nation.' These are the words which you shall speak to the children of Israel.

The Davidic Covenant
2 Samuel 7:12-17
"When your days are complete and you lie down with your fathers, I will raise up your descendant after you, who will come forth from you, and I will establish his kingdom. He shall build a house for My name, and I will establish the throne of his kingdom forever. I will be a father to him and he will be a son to Me; when he commits iniquity, I will correct him with the rod of men and the strokes of the sons of men, but My lovingkindness shall not depart from him, as I took *it* away from Saul, whom I removed from before you. Your house and your kingdom shall endure before Me forever; your throne shall be established forever." In accordance with all these words and all this vision, so Nathan spoke to David.

The New Covenant
Jeremiah 31:31-34
"Behold, the days are coming, says the LORD, when I will make a new covenant with the house of Israel and with the house of Judah— not according to the covenant that I made with their fathers in the day that I took them by the hand to lead them out of the land of Egypt, My covenant which they broke, though I was a husband to them, says the LORD. But this is the covenant that I will make with the house of Israel after those days, says the LORD: I will put My law in their minds, and write it on their hearts; and I will be their God, and they shall be My people. No more shall every man teach his neighbor, and every man his brother, saying, 'Know the LORD,' for they all shall know Me, from the least of them to the greatest of them, says the LORD. For I will forgive their iniquity, and their sin I will remember no more."

The Seven Pillars of Wisdom

The seven pillars of wisdom are established in Proverbs 8 and 9.

Proverbs 8:12-14: I wisdom dwell with prudence, and find out knowledge of witty inventions. The fear of the LORD is to hate evil: pride, and arrogancy, and the evil way, and the froward mouth, do I hate. Counsel is mine, and sound wisdom: I am understanding; I have strength.

Proverbs 9:1: Wisdom hath builded her house, she hath hewn out her seven pillars.

Proverbs 9:10: "The fear of the LORD is the beginning of wisdom, And the knowledge of the Holy One is understanding.

Seven Pillars of Wisdom
Prudence
Sound Judgment
Knowledge and Discretion
Insight
Fear of the Lord
Power
Counsel

The Twelve Tribes of Israel

Reuben
Simeon
Levi
Judah
Issachar
Zebulon
Naphtali
Gad
Asher
Benjamin
Ephraim
Manasseh

Note: Dan was one of the 12 tribes, but was later removed because of their repeated falls into idolatry.

Note: Joseph was replaced by his two sons Ephraim and Manasseh.

Note: All of the tribes of Israel descended from Jacob.
Below, you will find the mothers of each of Jacob's sons.

Leah	**Rachel**	**Zilpah**	**Bilhah**
Reuben	Joseph	Gad	Dan
Simeon	Benjamin	Asher	Naphtali
Levi			
Judah			
Issachar			
Zebulon			

Old Testament Books

S	X	S	N	L	E	V	I	T	I	C	U	S	R	D	D	Q
K	T	E	A	N	O	H	Q	F	I	C	M	U	L	O	M	C
B	F	C	J	N	A	O	F	I	A	L	R	V	E	W	P	S
A	I	O	S	G	M	D	I	R	A	Q	M	H	X	K	R	B
B	R	N	E	T	K	M	Z	S	U	Z	M	U	V	E	O	Z
V	S	D	C	G	R	E	P	T	J	T	V	Y	B	J	V	F
Q	T	C	O	E	N	A	R	C	P	Y	H	M	Y	P	E	I
O	S	H	N	N	J	O	S	H	U	A	U	E	M	I	R	R
U	A	R	D	E	U	T	E	R	O	N	O	M	Y	N	B	S
Z	M	O	K	S	D	L	S	O	I	E	D	R	C	B	S	T
I	U	N	I	I	G	Z	T	N	A	H	A	C	K	W	V	K
J	E	I	N	S	E	F	H	I	R	E	K	N	M	U	Q	I
V	L	C	G	S	S	Y	E	C	L	M	L	E	G	Z	Q	N
R	H	L	S	V	N	M	R	L	O	I	S	T	X	I	N	G
A	Q	E	M	O	C	T	E	E	Y	A	V	Y	G	B	F	S
V	N	S	E	X	O	D	U	S	K	H	T	Q	P	D	T	A
K	K	D	B	S	E	C	O	N	D	S	A	M	U	E	L	I

Deuteronomy
Esther
Exodus
Ezra
First Chronicles
First Kings
First Samuel
Genesis
Job
Joshua
Judges
Leviticus
Nehemiah
Numbers
Proverbs
Psalms
Ruth
Second Chronicles
Second Kings
Second Samuel

Old Testament Books (Second Half)

K	U	R	V	H	B	N	N	P	O	V	X	A	G	O	K	U
D	P	L	A	M	E	N	T	A	T	I	O	N	S	B	M	O
F	Q	N	P	T	N	S	Z	E	P	H	A	N	I	A	H	L
H	O	S	E	A	H	A	G	G	A	I	S	M	T	D	A	C
J	E	R	E	M	I	A	H	I	K	N	V	K	Z	I	B	K
U	O	U	G	E	M	A	R	U	Z	O	C	Y	F	A	A	N
M	W	E	I	K	C	A	H	V	M	U	L	P	V	H	K	U
B	Y	K	L	I	H	M	L	I	A	U	M	E	H	C	K	P
H	Z	Z	M	C	I	O	D	A	N	I	E	L	J	I	U	P
R	O	Q	E	O	E	S	Y	W	C	D	I	U	O	S	K	J
V	E	Z	E	K	I	E	L	E	P	H	T	V	V	W	Y	U
P	U	X	L	W	P	J	L	I	S	A	I	A	H	Y	M	M
W	Y	H	E	M	U	L	M	X	L	S	P	P	S	U	C	J
G	N	S	O	N	G	O	F	S	O	L	O	M	O	N	N	M
Q	X	E	C	C	L	E	S	I	A	S	T	E	S	Y	W	R
T	B	G	U	W	V	C	G	N	X	W	L	G	B	J	J	B
I	X	F	H	T	C	M	Z	E	L	Y	A	F	A	I	I	V

Amos
Daniel
Ecclesiastes
Ezekiel
Habakkuk
Haggai
Hosea
Isaiah
Jeremiah
Joel

Jonah
Lamentations
Micah
Nahum
Obadiah
Song of Solomon
Zechariah
Zephaniah
Malachi

Fruits of the Spirit vs. Works of the Flesh

Galatians 5:16-25
This I say then, Walk in the Spirit, and ye shall not fulfil the lust of the flesh. For the flesh lusteth against the Spirit, and the Spirit against the flesh: and these are contrary the one to the other: so that ye cannot do the things that ye would. But if ye be led of the Spirit, ye are not under the law. Now the works of the flesh are manifest, which are these; adultery, fornication, uncleanness, lasciviousness, idolatry, witchcraft, hatred, variance, emulations, wrath, strife, seditions, heresies, envyings, murders, drunkenness, revellings, and such like: of the which I tell you before, as I have also told you in time past, that they which do such things shall not inherit the kingdom of God. But the fruit of the Spirit is love, joy, peace, longsuffering, gentleness, goodness, faith, meekness, temperance: against such there is no law. And they that are Christ's have crucified the flesh with the affections and lusts. If we live in the Spirit, let us also walk in the Spirit.

17 Works of the Flesh		
Adultery	Fornication	Uncleanness
Lasciviousness	Idolatry	Witchcraft
Hatred	Variance	Emulations
Wrath	Strife	Sedition
Heresies	Envyings	Murders
Drunkenness		Revelings

Nine Fruits of the Spirit		
Love	Joy	Peace
Longsuffering	Gentleness	Goodness
Faith	Meekness	Temperance

God Gives Gifts!

Below, we will explore the gift-giving nature of God!

Ecclesiastes 3:13
And also that every man should eat and drink, and enjoy the good of all his labour, it is the gift of God.

1 Corinthians 12:4-11
Now there are diversities of gifts, but the same Spirit. And there are differences of administrations, but the same Lord. And there are diversities of operations, but it is the same God which worketh all in all. But the manifestation of the Spirit is given to every man to profit withal. For to one is given by the Spirit the word of wisdom; to another the word of knowledge by the same Spirit; To another faith by the same Spirit; to another the gifts of healing by the same Spirit; to another the working of miracles; to another prophecy; to another discerning of spirits; to another divers kinds of tongues; to another the interpretation of tongues: But all these worketh that one and the selfsame Spirit, dividing to every man severally as he will.

John 14:16-17
And I will pray the Father, and he shall give you another Comforter, that he may abide with you for ever; even the Spirit of truth; whom the world cannot receive, because it seeth him not, neither knoweth him: but ye know him; for he dwelleth with you, and shall be in you.

Gifts of the Spirit
Word of Wisdom
Word of Knowledge
Faith
Gifts of Healing
Working of Miracles
Prophecies
Discerning of Spirits
Diverse Tongues
Interpretation of Tongues

Ephesians 4:11-16
And he gave some, apostles; and some, prophets; and some, evangelists; and some, pastors and teachers; for the perfecting of the saints, for the work of the ministry, for the edifying of the body of Christ: Till we all come in the unity of the faith, and of the knowledge of the Son of God, unto a perfect man, unto the measure of the stature of the fulness of Christ: That we henceforth be no more children, tossed to and fro, and carried about with every wind of doctrine, by the sleight of men, and cunning craftiness, whereby they lie in wait to deceive; but speaking the truth in love, may grow up into him in all things, which is the head, even Christ: From whom the whole body fitly joined together and compacted by that which every joint supplieth, according to the effectual working in the measure of every part, maketh increase of the body unto the edifying of itself in love.

Five-Fold Gifts	Apostles	Prophets	Evangelists	Teachers	Pastors

Romans 5:15
But not as the offence, so also is the free gift. For if through the offence of one many be dead, much more the grace of God, and the gift by grace, which is by one man, Jesus Christ, hath abounded unto many.

Romans 6:23
For the wages of sin is death; but the gift of God is eternal life through Jesus Christ our Lord.

Note: this is NOT a complete list of the gifts God has given us!
Throughout the Bible, you'll witness God giving supernatural endowments to men and women, all of which are GIFTS, meaning, they did NOT deserve them!

DANGER!!!

One morning, a man woke up from a dream. In his dream, he saw himself preaching the Word of God to a crowd of people, but the problem with this was he was a parishioner or a minister at a church. He was not the lead pastor. He sat up on his bed and began to pray at God, instead of praying to Him. "Yes, Lord! I'll do it!" he shouted. "I'll answer the call!" Another issue had been brewing in his heart of hearts. He'd sat under his pastor for many years, and while he had ascended the ranks of ministry within his local assembly, he was still not the head pastor—not even close to it. At the same time, he'd been studying his Bible intensively and he'd been granted access to a realm of revelation that was not being taught in the church he attended. As a matter of fact, much of the revelation he'd acquired seemed to somewhat contradict what his pastor had been teaching, so one day, he decided to meet with his pastor and share his concerns. The meeting didn't go as planned and the man immediately resigned from the church. A few months later, he announced publicly that he was starting his own church, and this church would be filled with untaught truths and never-before heard revelation. Some of the members from his former church attended his church, and before long he'd acquired a relatively decent-sized congregation. But what could they call themselves? How could they differentiate themselves from other churches and denominations? After all, they were teaching a truth or a doctrine that no other church had been teaching. It didn't take long for him to come up with a title for his new denomination! He registered it and membership continued to grow.

A few years later, one of his members had an encounter with God and he too believed that he had a measure of knowledge and revelation that had never before been shared with mankind. Like his predecessor, he eventually left his church and started his own denomination. This pattern repeated itself until we one day looked up and saw the members of Christ dismembered and scattered about the Earth, arguing over minuscule things, all claiming to be right, while their brethren (according to them) were not only wrong, but heretic and hell-bound. But how does that work? Why would God give these men dreams and encounters? Was it the will of God for them to take the revelation and start their own churches or denominations? Before I answer this question, let's build using the scriptures!

Ephesians 4:9-16
Now that he ascended, what is it but that he also descended first into the lower parts of the earth? He that descended is the same also that ascended up far above all heavens, that he might fill all things.) And he gave some, apostles; and some, prophets; and some, evangelists; and some, pastors and teachers; for the perfecting of the saints, for the work of the ministry, for the edifying of the body of Christ: Till we all come in the unity of the faith, and of the knowledge of the Son of God, unto a perfect man, unto the measure of the stature of the fulness of Christ: That we henceforth be no more children, tossed to and fro, and carried about with every wind of doctrine, by the sleight of men, and cunning craftiness, whereby they lie in wait to deceive; but speaking the truth in love, may grow up into him in all things, which is the head, even Christ: From whom the whole body fitly joined together and compacted by that which every joint supplieth, according to the effectual working in the measure of every part, maketh increase of the body unto the edifying of itself in love.

Our job or assignment is to mature in the things of God. The response of maturity is unity. Pride, selfish conceit and ambition are the divisive tools that Satan uses to divide the church. So, the goal is to mature, and the evidence of this maturity is unity. Now that we've established this fact, let's look at another scripture.

Acts 2:17-21
And it shall come to pass in the last days, saith God, I will pour out of my Spirit upon all flesh: and your sons and your daughters shall prophesy, and your young men shall see visions, and your old men shall dream dreams: And on my servants and on my handmaidens I will pour out in those days of my Spirit; and they shall prophesy: And I will shew wonders in heaven above, and signs in the earth beneath; blood, and fire, and vapour of smoke: The sun shall be turned into darkness, and the moon into blood, before that great and notable day of the Lord come: And it shall come to pass, that whosoever shall call on the name of the Lord shall be saved.

God said that in the last days, He would pour out His Spirit on all flesh. Now, I want you to imagine a woman sitting on the back row of a church during service. All of a sudden, the Spirit of God begins to express Himself through her, and she begins to prophesy. The prophetic word that she's sharing has never before been heard at her church. The people are astonished, and most of the congregation falls upon their faces and begins to repent. Does this mean that she should start her own church? Of course not! It means that she is a part of the body of Christ and God is using her to edify the members. Her goal isn't to dismember the body, but to further unify it. Howbeit, if pride and selfish ambition are to creep in, she will find herself prophesying in the parking lot, hoping to win the hearts of the people so that she can start her own church or potentially start her own denomination. Let's look at one more scripture for this lesson!

1 Corinthians 13:9
For we know in part, and we prophesy in part.

We are parts or, better yet, members of the body of Christ. God gives those of us who pursue Him a peak into who He is. This sneak-peak is called revelation. When this happens, our assignment is to bring that revelation to the body of Christ so that the members can unify or come together all the more and mature! But the problem that arose is that, instead of people doing this, they opted to treat ministry as a business; they dismembered the body of Christ for selfish gain, and thus, we witnessed the birth of denominations!

The obvious question is, “What if the pastor was a heretic? What if he was teaching falsehoods to a group of hungry people? Should someone who has a revelation of the truth continue to sit there, or should that person launch his own church or congregation?” The answer to this question may shock some, offend some, intrigue some and mature some. His job was to pray and wait. His job was to follow biblical protocol; he was to go to his leader and express what he'd heard God saying and also ask questions, if needed. His job was to wait for God to respond. You see, whatever word he received (if it came from God) was for the congregation that he was a part of. Every church and congregation has a specific diet carefully crafted by God to help them power through the strongholds of that particular region. When the man in question decided to leave his church, he decided to personally attribute the revelation to himself, thus, stealing the glory of God for his own selfish gain. And through denominationalism, he scattered the sheep. And now, many denominations have a true Word from God that is designed for the members of their regions, but they are scattered, so one church gets a piece of the puzzle, while the neighboring church has another piece. When these pieces come together, they form the picture of God. Then again, many denominations have a true Word from God that is designed for the body of Christ in its entirety, but again, because we are divided in our beliefs and further divided by our cultures, there is no way for us to communicate the heart of God throughout the Earth. Consequently, our next set of instructions from Heaven is oftentimes delayed because of division.

1 Corinthians 1:11-17
For it hath been declared unto me of you, my brethren, by them which are of the house of Chloe, that there are contentions among you. Now this I say, that every one of you saith, I am of Paul; and I of Apollos; and I of Cephas; and I of Christ. Is Christ divided? Was Paul crucified for you? Or were ye baptized in the name of Paul? I thank God that I baptized none

of you, but Crispus and Gaius; Lest any should say that I had baptized in mine own name. And I baptized also the household of Stephanas: besides, I know not whether I baptized any other. For Christ sent me not to baptize, but to preach the gospel: not with wisdom of words, lest the cross of Christ should be made of none effect.

What Apostle Paul was dealing with here was what could have potentially become the division of the church into denominations. These types of conversations and lines of reasoning are rooted in pride, and pride always divides anything that it enters! Church splits and denominationalism are almost always the result of offense, pride and human ambition! Of course, not all denominations are the result of a man or woman hearing from God and leaving their churches. Some are the direct result of wolves in sheep's clothing launching ministry-based businesses and gangs. To date, there are over 45,000 denominations of Christianity or, better yet, 45,000 splits in the body of Christ, some of which are truly His people, while others are knowingly or unknowingly polytheistic. In other words, they worship their pastors, their doctrines and they mask their idolatry by using Christian terminology. Of these 45,000 denominations, there are many sects (sections or sectors), most of which split because of some person's desire to start his or her own ministry. And to ensure that the body of Christ does not regroup or "remember," Satan promotes pride and offense.

Below are the six dangers of denominationalism:

1. **Satan's goal is to divide and conquer!** The Bible tells us that Satan goes about looking for whom he can devour. Think of it this way. You can't shove an entire steak in your mouth! In order to eat and truly savor it, you would have to cut it into small pieces and eat each chunk one by one. This is what Satan has done to the church! He divided us so that he could devour us!
2. **Denominationalism allows us to hear one side of a prophecy, without being able to see the other side of it.** We prophesy in part! Believe it or not, the answer to most (if not all) of this world's problems is scattered all over the Earth, being held captive by men and women who want to copyright it.
3. **Denominationalism or division teaches the sheep that division is okay if they can come up with a religious-enough excuse for their rebellion.** We can't teach or encourage the sheep to stay in our churches if we ourselves are serving as fragmented parts of the body of Christ.
4. **Denominationalism further confuses the sheep and makes it difficult for unbelievers to surrender their lives to Christ.** Unbelievers who desire a relationship with God are oftentimes scared off by the menu of choices that they have to choose from. With every denomination claiming to be right, unbelievers and some believers alike find themselves overwhelmed by the many voices, all of which claim to be disciples of Jesus.

5. **Denominationalism produces pride**, and pride poisons the perspective of the sheep, therefore, making it difficult for them to live long, productive, abundant and joy-filled lives! In order for one man to say, "I am of Cephas," and another to say, "I was baptized by Apollos," each man has to think higher of himself than he ought to; this is the very pulse of pride!
6. **Denominationalism stunts the growth of the sheep!** While the shepherds get fatter, the sheep begin to devour one another in an attempt to fill their voids.

Acts 4:31-35
And when they had prayed, the place was shaken where they were assembled together; and they were all filled with the Holy Ghost, and they spake the word of God with boldness. And the multitude of them that believed were of one heart and of one soul: neither said any of them that ought of the things which he possessed was his own; but they had all things common. And with great power gave the apostles witness of the resurrection of the Lord Jesus: and great grace was upon them all. Neither was there any among them that lacked: for as many as were possessors of lands or houses sold them, and brought the prices of the things that were sold, And laid them down at the apostles' feet: and distribution was made unto every man according as he had need.

This scripture dealt with possessions, but the same concept applies to knowledge, revelation and understanding! God shares His heart with us, not so that we can keep it to ourselves, but so that we can publish His thoughts for His people! Can you imagine how powerful the church at large would be if the members all obeyed God and published the books, the blogs, the inventions and the businesses that He's given them? Could you imagine how potent the church at large would be if after publishing a book or launching a business, the members didn't get prideful and leave their churches in search for platforms to fit their over-sized pride? Could you imagine the dominion the church would walk in if we stopped allowing offense to be our god?! We were never created to hoard revelation!

So, where should you go? What denomination is right, and who is wrong? The answer is simple. Study your Bible and ask God to lead you! After that, visit some churches until you hear or sense God confirming that you're in the right place! And understand this—your pastor isn't going to be perfect or all-knowing! His or her assignment is to lead; your assignment is to follow and bring whatever revelation or knowledge God entrusts you with to your local assembly! Your job is to submit it to leadership! And if you follow the heart, will and mind of God, you will see people getting healed, delivered and saved because of your obedience!

LOSS EQUALS GAIN

3 - 2 = 1

FATHER
SON
HOLY SPIRIT

What's up in the world's system is down in the Kingdom. What's good to the world is evil to the Lord. What the world considers to be strength, the Word calls weakness. And what we consider to be gain in the world is loss in the Kingdom. Our world is parallel to the Kingdom of God, and because of this, we see things from an inverted perspective.

Philippians 3:7
But what things were gain to me, those I counted loss for Christ.

Proverbs 14:12
There is a way which seemeth right unto a man, but the end thereof are the ways of death.

Mark 8:36
For what shall it profit a man, if he shall gain the whole world, and lose his own soul?

Matthew 16:25
For whosoever will save his life shall lose it: and whosoever will lose his life for my sake shall find it.

Throughout the scriptures, we see men who've lost it all for God's sake (literally), only to have it restored. Consider the story of Job.

Beginning (Loss)	End (Gain)
Again, there was a day when the sons of God came to present themselves before the LORD, and Satan came also among them to present himself before the LORD. And the LORD said unto Satan, From whence comest thou? And Satan answered the LORD, and said, from going to and fro in the earth, and from walking up and down in it. And the LORD said unto Satan, Hast thou considered my servant Job, that there is none like him in the earth, a perfect and an upright man, one that feareth God, and escheweth evil? and still he holdeth fast his integrity, although thou movedst me against him, to destroy him without cause. And Satan answered the LORD, and said, Skin for skin, yea, all that a man hath will he give for his life. But put forth thine hand now, and touch his bone and his flesh, and he will curse thee to thy face. And the LORD said unto Satan, Behold, he *is* in thine hand; but save his life.	And the LORD turned the captivity of Job, when he prayed for his friends: also, the LORD gave Job twice as much as he had before. Then came there unto him all his brethren, and all his sisters, and all they that had been of his acquaintance before, and did eat bread with him in his house: and they bemoaned him, and comforted him over all the evil that the LORD had brought upon him: every man also gave him a piece of money, and everyone an earring of gold. So, the LORD blessed the latter end of Job more than his beginning: for he had fourteen thousand sheep, and six thousand camels, and a thousand yoke of oxen, and a thousand she asses. He had also seven sons and three daughters. And he called the name of the first, Jemima; and the name of the second, Kezia; and the name of the third, Kerenhappuch. And in all the land were no women found so fair as the daughters of Job: and their father gave them inheritance among their brethren. After this lived Job an hundred and forty years, and saw his sons, and his sons' sons, even four generations. So, Job died, being old and full of days.
Job 1:2-6	**Job 42:10-17**

Let's compare the beginning of Job's (tangible) blessings to the end. Please note that what we refer to as the end is nothing but a new beginning.

Beginning (Loss)	End (Gain)
7 sons, 3 Daughters	7 sons, 3 Daughters
7,000 Sheep	14,000 Sheep

Beginning (Loss)	End (Gain)
3,000 Camels	6,000 Camels
500 Yoke of Oxen	1,000 Yoke of Oxen
500 Donkeys	1,000 Donkeys

The Ground of Revelation

Matthew 13:3-10
And he spake many things unto them in parables, saying, Behold, a sower went forth to sow; and when he sowed, some seeds fell by the way side, and the fowls came and devoured them up: Some fell upon stony places, where they had not much earth: and forthwith they sprung up, because they had no deepness of earth: And when the sun was up, they were scorched; and because they had no root, they withered away. And some fell among thorns; and the thorns sprung up, and choked them: But other fell into good ground, and brought forth fruit, some an hundredfold, some sixtyfold, some thirtyfold. Who hath ears to hear, let him hear.

Matthew 13:18-23 (ESV)
Hear then the parable of the sower: When anyone hears the word of the kingdom and does not understand it, the evil one comes and snatches away what has been sown in his heart. This is what was sown along the path. As for what was sown on rocky ground, this is the one who hears the word and immediately receives it with joy, yet he has no root in himself, but endures for a while, and when tribulation or persecution arises on account of the word, immediately he falls away. As for what was sown among thorns, this is the one who hears the word, but the cares of the world and the deceitfulness of riches choke the word, and it proves unfruitful. As for what was sown on good soil, this is the one who hears the word and understands it. He indeed bears fruit and yields, in one case a hundredfold, in another sixty, and in another thirty.

Four Types of Hearers			
The Simp	**The Hardhearted**	**The Perverted**	**The Fruitful**
Lacks Understanding	Lacks Faith	Lacks Integrity	Faithful, Wise and Integral
When anyone hears the word of the kingdom and does not understand it, the evil one comes and snatches away what has been sown in his heart.	As for what was sown on rocky ground, this is the one who hears the word and immediately receives it with joy, yet he has no root in himself, but endures for a while, and when tribulation or persecution arises on account of the word, immediately he falls away.	As for what was sown among thorns, this is the one who hears the word, but the cares of the world and the deceitfulness of riches choke the word, and it proves unfruitful.	As for what was sown on good soil, this is the one who hears the word and understands it. He indeed bears fruit and yields, in one case a hundredfold, in another sixty, and in another thirty.

In this lineup of characters, it is important for you to identify what type of hearer you are; this way, if you need development in a certain area, you can intentionally target that particular area. And hear me—if you are not yet fruitful, you have nothing to be ashamed of! Maybe you were never taught to bear or maintain fruit.

One of the first laws of deliverance is that you have to admit or acknowledge where you are!

The Simp
Proverbs 4:7
Wisdom is the principal thing; therefore get wisdom: and with all thy getting get understanding.

Let's look at wisdom, knowledge and understanding dimensionally.

Knowledge	Topsoil
Understanding	Subsoil
Wisdom	Bedrock
Revelation	

Wisdom is the foundation.

It is the most important part of any structure. Proverbs 3:19, "The LORD by wisdom hath founded the earth; by understanding hath he established the heavens." Knowledge, on the other hand, rests on the surface of our minds. It eventually seeps into our hearts through a process of meditations and repetitions. It's the information that we learn and accept to be true or render to be false. The more we accept something to be true, the deeper it roots itself. This is why the Bible tells us to study and show ourselves approved! The more we study, the bigger the garden. Remember, the dust represents our skin-nature, but the problem is, sin intermingled with our flesh so now, we are wrestling with our sin-nature! Our goal is to overwhelm our minds with knowledge until we have enough know-how to defeat the debris (sin) that makes us dirty (sinful)! So, when God shares information or revelation with the Simp, the problem is, he has no root or depth to receive this information. He's a learner, but not a student or a doer of the Word. He's emotionally driven; he loves to hear the prophetic word going forth, he loves intense moments of corporate worship, but at home, he doesn't have a study life. He doesn't search out the scriptures. By the time he leaves church, he's forgotten most of what his pastor taught that day. He's never set the groundwork for understanding, so he has enough ground (capacity) to receive knowledge, but no depth to grow it. Consequently, this is what the Simp looks like to God.

Knowledge	Topsoil
Hard Heart	Bedrock

When revelation or knowledge hits the bedroom, it lacks the depth needed to grow roots. It is because of this that every time he learns something new, Satan sees it resting on the topsoil of his heart and is able to steal it with ease.

The Hardhearted

Every pastor is familiar with this character! This is the easily offended, overly emotional, entitled and spiritually bipolar believer who excitedly runs after prophecies, platforms and affirmation! Notice when the scripture describes this believer, the author details two dynamics:

1. He receives the word with JOY!
2. When affliction or persecution arises for the Word's sake, this believer is immediately OFFENDED (see KJV).

This is why I said this particular believer is spiritually bipolar. When they love their church or their pastor, they LOVE their church and their pastor! But when they are offended, they HATE their church and their pastor with the same intensity that they once loved them! Hear me—persecution WILL arise because of the Word that you carry! But if you cannot endure the persecution without quitting, gossiping or allowing offense to start bossing you around, you will fall under this category! Look at the setup of this particular believer below!

Wisdom	Bedrock
Understanding	Subsoil
Knowledge	Topsoil

What's different about this particular believer? What do you notice about the chart? It's turned upside down! This is why the scriptures refer to their hearts as rocky ground! The hardhearted, prideful or easily offended believer is what we call a wise guy. This character is wise in his/her own eyes and too hardhearted to receive correction. People like this want to be deep; they want attention and platforms, but they are not avid students of the Word. They study enough to remember a few of their favorite scriptures, but nothing is ever able to truly take root within them because their hearts are like bedrock. They ran after the pulpits before they ran towards the pews, and consequently, they have no knowledge or understanding, but they do have a lot of wise quotes and they've learned to mimic their favorite preachers' personalities. Because of this, they are easily offended and extremely emotional. When they're up, they're up; when they're down, they want to bring everyone else down with them!

The Perverted

Before we dig into this particular believer, let's first understand this—the word "perverted" is a multifaceted term, so it doesn't just deal with sexual perversion. There are many branches of perversion. To be perverted means to be twisted in your thinking.

"As for what was sown among thorns, this is the one who hears the word, but the cares of the world and the deceitfulness of riches choke the word, and it proves unfruitful." Earlier on, we established what the word "thorn" metaphorically represents.

Thorns (Flesh)	Thistles (Mind)
Perversions	Strongholds

Notice that the scripture said the revelation was sown among thorns. Have you ever seen a thorny plant in a garden or in a field? Chances are, you have! And if so, what you should have noticed is that thorny plants tend to wrap themselves up together and around other plants. They are truly twisted, and for the ones that don't twist, they're just painfully abrasive! This particular believer has it all:

Knowledge	Topsoil
Understanding	Subsoil
Wisdom	Bedrock
Revelation	

But the problem with this particular believer is that he's still in love with the world. Gardens are a place of order; wildernesses, on the other hand, are places of disorder. This believer professes to be a garden (believer), but looks and behaves more like a forest (unbeliever). Believers like this will study, come to church (sometimes) and even become pillars of a movement, but those weeds and thorns are slowly but surely taking over their minds. Their thoughts are perverted; they fantasize about platforms, power and success. They are not truly interested in helping people unless; that is, a camera is pointed at them or they can blog about it. Many of them truly have a heart for Jesus, but their perversions have slowly began to consume their lives and their focus! These people leave one church to join another just because the personality at the other church has a seemingly bigger platform than the churches they once committed themselves to. They're anointed, impatient and they will latch onto anyone who prophetically or personally affirms them. Again, this is why the scriptures refer to them as thorns. They are twisted in their thinking, irrational, unreasonable and eventually, they become unreliable!

The Fruitful

This is what we call good ground! This is what we call solid ground! These are the believers who trust God enough to let Him prune them! To prune is to correct, to circumcise and to stretch, none of which are pleasant experiences! God has weeded out the thistles and the thorns in their lives, and even though they're still waiting on the blessings to blossom in many areas in their lives, they still trust God!

Knowledge	Topsoil
Understanding	Subsoil
Wisdom	Bedrock
Revelation	

These types of believers take knowledge and peel away at its layers until they have extracted all of its nutrients and vitamins! They take everything that's given to them and multiply it! This is why they are called faithful sons and daughters of the Most High God! They aren't just hearers of the Word, they are doers of the Word! And it is for this reason that God grants them access into revelation! Like every other believer, they deal with their fair share of offense, frustration and every other temptation underneath the sun, but they don't serve their feelings; they make their feelings serve them! This is why God trusts them! When they're offended, they forgive; when they're scared, they pray; when they're overwhelmed, they refresh themselves! Satan has thrown every dart he can find at them, but they are too headstrong to die! Satan stole their friends and most of the people in their circles, and this only taught them to love themselves! If they don't understand something, they study and ask questions! They lead when no one is following, and they know who to follow when everyone else seems to be leading! They don't chase behind the biggest platforms or personalities; they are not entitled or anxious! Instead, they are humble, reliable, consistent and disciplined! The fruits of the Holy Spirit blossom in their lives in every season! This is because they are products of God's power. Remember, potential, once it is actualized, is no longer potential, it becomes powerful! These are the fruitful servants of God! Look at the chart below! This is what a believer like this looks like! They are repeatedly producing fruit because they maintain order in their lives!

Love	Joy	Peace
Longsuffering	Gentleness	Goodness
Faith	Meekness	Temperance

Knowledge	Topsoil
Understanding	Subsoil
Wisdom	Bedrock

Which type of believer are you? It's important for you to know where you are so that you can get whatever it is you need for you to grow. The ground of revelation is rich and ready for believers to tap into it, but it takes someone who understands that there is a level of warfare and persecution that comes with being doers and keepers of the Word!

Challenge

Identify what type of believer you are!

Write a note to your mentor or pastor identifying the type of believer that you are, listing the areas where you need to grow in the most. After this, create a six-week plan, detailing the steps that you will take to faciliate this growth. Be as detailed as possible. If there's not enough room on the next page to list your plan, simply use a separate document or sheet of paper.

SIX WEEK PLAN

Week One

Week Two

Week Three

Week Four

Week Five

Week Six

Aaron's Ephod

Exodus 28:15-22
And thou shalt make the breastplate of judgment with cunning work; after the work of the ephod thou shalt make it; of gold, of blue, and of purple, and of scarlet, and of fine twined linen, shalt thou make it. Foursquare it shall be being doubled; a span shall be the length thereof, and a span shall be the breadth thereof. And thou shalt set in it settings of stones, even four rows of stones: the first row shall be a sardius, a topaz, and a carbuncle: this shall be the first row. And the second row shall be an emerald, a sapphire, and a diamond. And the third row a ligure, an agate, and an amethyst. And the fourth row a beryl, and an onyx, and a jasper: they shall be set in gold in their inclosings. And the stones shall be with the names of the children of Israel, twelve, according to their names, like the engravings of a signet; everyone with his name shall they be according to the twelve tribes. And thou shalt make upon the breastplate chains at the ends of wreathen work of pure gold.

Sardius	Topaz	Carbuncle	Emerald	Sapphire	Diamond
REUBEN	SIMEON	LEVI	EMERALD	ISSACHAR	ZEBULUN
Ligure	**Agate**	**Amethyst**	**Beryl**	**Onyx**	**Jasper**
NEPHTALI	GAD	ASHER	MANASSAH	EPHRAM	BENJAMIN

2 Samuel 6:14
And David danced before the LORD with all his might; and David was girded with a linen ephod.

1 Samuel 23:9
And David knew that Saul secretly practised mischief against him; and he said to Abiathar the priest, Bring hither the ephod.

Branches of Reformation

Anglicanism
Founded by King Henry VIII in 134, Anglicanism is a doctrine established on the belief that God has chosen an elect group of people to receive salvation. Anglicans believe that salvation is not available for anyone outside of the people God has chosen before He created mankind. King Henry VIII didn't want to share his power with the church, so he made himself the head of the church; this was because he wanted to divorce his wife and marry another woman, but the Catholic church forbid this. Anglican beliefs are a hybrid between Catholicism and Protestantism.

Baptism
Doctrine established by the belief that salvation is attained through the full immersion of a person's body in water in baptism. Baptists do not have a governing authority like the Catholic or Anglican church. Note: not all Baptists believe that baptism is a requirement for salvation. Like many other Christian denominations, beliefs vary from church to church.

Calvinism
Belief in sanctification and predestination. In short, Calvinists believe that the elect (those who would be saved) were chosen before birth to obtain salvation. Calvinists refer to themselves as reformed Catholics. Calvinists based their beliefs on how their monarch interpreted the Bible.

Lutheranism
Established by Martin Luther, a German reformer, Lutherans split from the Catholic Church, being divided on the beliefs of authority in the church and the doctrine of justification. Martin Luther had been ex-communicated by the Catholic Church, so he established Lutheranism.

Pentecostalism
Derived from the Pentecost, Pentecostalism is a doctrine established on the belief that salvation is attained through baptism of the Holy Spirit.

HOW TO STUDY THE BIBLE

How to Study the Bible

Preparation

Number One: Find a place that ACTIVATES your ears.

Quiet Place
Coffee Shop
Grocery Store
Office

Number Two: Find your weapon of choice.

"Version" vs. "Translation"
Over 50 English versions
King James
New King James
American Standard
Amplified
New International
New Living

See next page for a short list of Bible versions.

Short List of Bible Versions

King James Version	New American Standard Version	The Message
New International Version	Young's Literal Translation	New Jerusalem Bible
Revised Standard Version	Plain English Bible	Hebrew Names Version of World English Bible
The Living Bible	New English Bible	Contemporary English Version
New Living Translation	Amplified Bible	English Version for the Deaf
World English Bible	Basic English Bible	Good News Version
New King James Version	Translator's NT	New Century Version
New International Readers Editions	20th Century Bible	New Revised Standard Version
American Standard Version	Modern King James Version	J. B. Phillips New Testament, Modern English

Number Three: Get to know the Author.

Own a Bible
Be planted in a church
Attend regularly
Develop a prayer regime
Worship should be your life source

2 Timothy 2:15
Study to shew thyself approved unto God, a workman that needeth not to be ashamed, rightly dividing the word of truth.

THE CANON OF SCRIPTURE

- "Canon" means a "rule, measuring stick, a standard, or model."
- A book labeled as canonical has met the standard, or rule, as the inspired Word of God.
- The Apocrypha (hidden or concealed) did not appear in a Bible until the Council of Trent in 1546 A.D.

Non-Canonical Books	
Book of Jasher	Book of Shemaiah and Iddo, the Seer
The Book of the Wars of the Lord	Books of Chronicles
Book of Enoch	The Book of Nathan the Prophet
Gnostic Gospels	The Book of Samuel, the Seer
Gospel of Thomas	The Manner of the Kingdom
Gospel of Mary	The Acts of Solomon
Chronicles of the Kings of Israel/ Chronicles of the Kings of Judah	The Annals of King David
Book of Gad, the Seer	The Prophecy of Ahijah
Book of Jehu	The Story of the Books of Kings
Acts of Uzziah	Vision of Isaiah
The Acts of the Kings of Israel	The Sayings of the Seers
Laments for Josiah	The Chronicles of King Ahasuerus

14 Books of Apocrypha

1 Esdras	2 Esdras	Tobit	Judith	Rest of Esther
Wisdom	Ecclesiasticus (Sirach	Baruch	Song of the Three Children	Story of Susanna
The Idol Bel and the Dragon	Prayer of Manasseh		1 Maccabees	2 Maccabees

The Books called the Apocrypha consist of 14 books. These books had been attached to the Old Testament (Greek), but theye were not in the Hebrew Bible. The reason for this is because they were weritten in Greek. Initially, they had been considered to be scriptures and were used by Jews who lived abroad (outside of Jerusalem); these Jews were referenced as Jews of the Dispersion. hey were considered scripture and used as such by Jews diaspora (Jews living in foreign countries) at the time of Christ. Eventually, any and all scriptural text that was not originally written in Hebrew was judged to be unclean and discarded.

Apocryphal: of doubtful authenticity: spurious (Source: Merriam Webster)
Origin: Apo (Greek): meaning away from or apart
This is where we get the word apostasy

Challenge

What have you heard about the non-canonical books of the Bible and/or the Apocryphal? What are your beliefs regarding these books, and why? Do not answer based on what you've heard! Before answering this question, please do some extensive research.

Your Answer

More Bible Facts

Total Books in the King James Bible **66**	Total Chapters in the King James Bible **1,189**	Total Verses in the King James Bible **31,102**
Total Books in the Old Testament **39**	Total Chapters in the Old Testament **929**	Total Verses in the Old Testament **23,145**
Total Books in the New Testament **27**	Total Chapters in the New Testament **260**	Total Verses in the New Testament **7,957**
Middle Book in the King James Bible **Micah & Nahum**	Longest Book in the King James Bible **Psalms**	Shortest Book in the King James Bible **2 John (verses) & 3 John**
Middle Chapter in the King James Bible **Psalm 117**	Longest Chapter in the King James Bible **Psalm 119**	Shortest Chapter in the King James Bible **Psalm 117**
Middle Verse in the King James Bible **Psalm 103:1 & Psalm 103:2**	Longest Verse in the King James Bible **Esther 8:9**	Shortest Verse in the King James Bible **John 11:35**

Overview
66 Books in the Bible
39 Old Testament
5 Books of Moses
12 Books of History (Joshua to Esther)
5 Books of Poetry (Job to Song of Solomon)
17 Books of Prophecy (Isaiah to Malachi)
27 New Testament Books
The Council of Carthage, 397 A.D. said “Nothing shall be read in the churches except the recognized canon”
4 Gospels (3 Synoptic)

Synoptic- of or forming a general summary or synopsis:
1 Book of History (Acts of the Apostles)
22 Epistles (Letters)
2 Corinthians 3:1-6

HOW THE WORD OF GOD IS RELEASED!!!

Seven Dimensions of the Word	
Water	For the husband is the head of the wife, even as Christ is the head of the church: and he is the Savior of the body. Ephesians 5:23
Milk	As newborn babes, desire the sincere milk of the word, that ye may grow thereby: If so be ye have tasted that the Lord is gracious. 1 Peter 2:2-3
Bread	So the priest gave him hallowed bread: for there was no bread there but the shewbread, that was taken from before the LORD, to put hot bread in the day when it was taken away. 1 Samuel 21:6
Meat	I have fed you with milk, and not with meat: for hitherto ye were not able to bear it, neither yet now are ye able. 1 Corinthians 3:2
Mystery	For we wrestle not against flesh and blood, but against principalities, against powers, against the rulers of the darkness of this world, against spiritual wickedness in high places. Ephesians 6:12
Corn	And it came to pass, that he went through the corn fields on the sabbath day; and his disciples began, as they went, to pluck the ears of corn. Mark 2:23
Honey	How sweet are thy words unto my taste! yea, sweeter than honey to my mouth! Psalm 119:103

The Word of God

Three Dimensions of the Word		
Graphe	**Logos**	**Rhema**
2 Timothy 3:16	*John 1:1*	*Ephesians 6:17*
All scripture is given by inspiration of God, and is profitable for doctrine, for reproof, for correction, for instruction in righteousness.	In the beginning was the Word, and the Word was with God, and the Word was God.	And take the helmet of salvation, and the sword of the Spirit, which is the word of God.

Inspiration vs. Revelation

a) Revelation- Revelation refers to something God has made known; He has unveiled, uncovered something. Proverbs 25:2

b) Inspiration- Inspiration refers to the transmission or the writing. It refers to the method that kept this writing from error or mistake.

Inspiration Produced the Bible, A Document of God's Self-Revelation

Moses, David, John, Paul were NOT always inspired. As men, they erred in conduct, but their fallibility and errancy were NEVER transmitted to the sacred writings. The Bible does NOT contain the Word of God, IT IS THE WORD OF GOD!!

Building Revelation

Moving from Information to Revelation

1 Corinthians 14:6
Now, brethren, if I come unto you speaking with tongues, what shall I profit you, except I shall speak to you either by revelation, or by knowledge, or by prophesying, or by doctrine?

Revelation Defined

Revelation: (Gr. Apokalupsis) - laying bear, making naked, a disclosure of truth, instruction, concerning things before unknown, withdrawn from view are made visible to all, manifestation, appearance.

Revelation (Def.): Something that is revealed by virtue of the Holy Spirit. Information disclosed at specific times for the purpose of acceleration.

Revelation of the House: The prevailing, understood will of God and its application, purpose, and direction for a particular church.

Revelation is only useful when it becomes RHEMA.

What is Rhema?

1. that which is or has been uttered by the living voice
2. any sound produced by the voice and having definite meaning
3. a series of words joined together into a sentence
4. declaration of one's mind made into words)
5. a matter of command

This is important because this means that once something is REVEALED, you have the responsibility to ADHERE to it.

SYMBOLS AND TYPES

Symbol: a word, phrase, image, or the like having a complex of associated meanings and perceived as having inherent value separable from that which is symbolized, as being part of that which is symbolized, and as performing its normal function of standing for or representing that which is symbolized: usually conceived as deriving its meaning chiefly from the structure in which it appears, and generally distinguished from a sign.

Symbolic Principle

It is that principle by which the interpretation of a verse or passage of scripture containing symbolic elements can be determined only by a proper interpretation of the symbols involved.

According to Webster's Dictionary, the word "symbol" is made up of two Greek words: "syn" meaning "together", and "ballein" meaning "to throw". It means literally "thrown together" and denotes an object used to represent something abstract: an emblem, using one thing to stand for another.

One of the major uses for the material realm is to symbolize and typify spiritual truth. For example, the Tabernacle of Moses and the Temple of Solomon. God instructed Moses to take things from various created kingdom to set forth symbolic truth.

The Four Kingdoms

Mineral Kingdom	Vegetable Kingdom	Animal Kingdom	Human Kingdom
Gold, silver and brass; precious stones, onyx stones for the ephod and breastplate.	Fine linen, shittim wood, olive oil for light, spices for the anointing, spices for the incense.	Clothes and dye, goat's hair, rams skin, sheep, oxen and birds.	Sons for priests, women for mirrors.

Classification of Symbols

Symbolic Objects	Psalm 18:2
Symbolic Creatures	Isaiah 40:31
Symbolic Actions	Psalm 141:1-2, Genesis 25:23-26, Joshua 1:3
Symbolic Numbers	2 Corinthians 13:1, Matthew 19:28
Symbolic Names	1 Samuel 4:21, Matthew 1:21
Symbolic Colors	Isaiah 1:18, Mark 15:17,18
Symbolic Directions	2 Chronicles 4:4, Ezekiel 43:1-2
Symbolic Places	Genesis 11:1-9, Hebrews 7:1-2

The Typical Principle

It is impossible to properly and fully interpret the scriptures without understanding TYPES.
Types: a thing or person that represents perfectly or in the best way a class or category; model.
Webster's Definition: An emblem; a symbol; that which has a symbolic significance; that which is emblematic.
Theologically, the word is mainly applied to those prophetic prefiguring of the persons and things of the new dispensation, which occur in the Old Testament.
The Typical Principle is that principle by which the interpretation of a verse or passage of scripture containing typical elements can be determined only through a proper interpretation of the type or types involved.

Types

Types can be translated as:

Print	John 20:25
Figure	Rom. 5:14
Fashion	Acts 7:44
Manner	Acts 23:25
Form	Romans 6:17
Example	1 Corinthians 10:6
Ensample	Philippians 3:17
Pattern	Hebrews 8:5

Types and Symbols

Symbol	a representation, one thing standing for another.
Type	a prophetic representation, one thing prefiguring another.
The ROCK in Psalms 18:2 is a symbol, not a type.	
The LAMB in John 1:29 is a symbol, not a type.	
ADAM in Romans 5:14 is a type, not a symbol.	
JONAH'S EXPERIENCE in the fish in Mt 12:39-41 is a type, not a symbol.	

Typical Persons	Typical Offices	Typical Institutions	Typical Events
Romans 5:12-21	Hebrews 5:1-10 (verse 4,5)	Hebrews 8:1-5	1 Corinthians 10:6, Genesis 22

Master Keys

The Tabernacle of Moses	The Feasts of the Lord	The Levitical Offerings
The Tabernacle of David	Day of Atonement	Aaronic and Levitical Priesthood
The Temple of Solomon		The Covenants of the Lord

Principles of Interpretation

The Context Principle	The Chronometrical Principle
The First Mention Principle	The Breach Principle
The Comparative Mention Principle	The Christo-Centric Principle
The Progressive Mention Principle	The Moral Principle
The Complete Mention Principle	The Symbolic Principle
The Election Principle	The Numerical Principle
The Covenantal Principle	The Typical Principle

Guidelines for Interpretation

Genesis 41:15-30

And Pharaoh said unto Joseph, I have dreamed a dream, and there is none that can interpret it: and I have heard say of thee, that thou canst understand a dream to interpret it. And Joseph answered Pharaoh, saying, it is not in me: God shall give Pharaoh an answer of peace. And Pharaoh said unto Joseph, In my dream, behold, I stood upon the bank of the river: And, behold, there came up out of the river seven kine, fatfleshed and well favoured;

and they fed in a meadow: And, behold, seven other kine came up after them, poor and very ill favoured and leanfleshed, such as I never saw in all the land of Egypt for badness: And the lean and the ill favoured kine did eat up the first seven fat kine: And when they had eaten them up, it could not be known that they had eaten them; but they were still ill favoured, as at the beginning. So, I awoke. And I saw in my dream, and, behold, seven ears came up in one stalk, full and good: And, behold, seven ears, withered, thin, and blasted with the east wind, sprung up after them: And the thin ears devoured the seven good ears: and I told this unto the magicians; but there was none that could declare it to me. And Joseph said unto Pharaoh, The dream of Pharaoh is one: God hath shewed Pharaoh what he is about to do. The seven good kine are seven years; and the seven good ears are seven years: the dream is one. And the seven thin and ill favoured kine that came up after them are seven years; and the seven empty ears blasted with the east wind shall be seven years of famine. This is the thing which I have spoken unto Pharaoh: What God is about to do he sheweth unto Pharaoh. Behold, there come seven years of great plenty throughout all the land of Egypt: And there shall arise after them seven years of famine; and all the plenty shall be forgotten in the land of Egypt; and the famine shall consume the land; and the plenty shall not be known in the land by reason of that famine following; for it shall be very grievous. And for that the dream was doubled unto Pharaoh twice; it is because the thing is established by God, and God will shortly bring it to pass.

Remember these guidelines for interpreting dreams:

- Before you interpret anyone's dream, try to interpret your own dreams.
- Your interpretation must have a strong Biblical foundation
- Interpretation is MEAT FUNCTION (for those on meat diet)
- Accountability structures (room to be wrong)
- 1 Corinthians 12: Interpretation of tongues

Steps to Dream Interpretation

Number One: Make a note so you won't forget.

Dreams are imprinted, sealed, and engraved through the writing process.
WRITE, WRITE, WRITE!

Number Two: Understand that most dreams are symbolic.

Dreams require interpretation!, and then, prophetic action, which is initiated by WORDS OF WISDOM!

Number Three: Pray and ask God to reveal the meaning to you.
Prayer unlocks vaults of revelation, while removing layers of understanding. 1. Prophetic Prayer: Warning signs that produce prayers of URGENCY 2. Power Prayer: It takes consistency to birth dreams BIRTHING PANGS 3. Pray the Scripture (Matthew 4) The Temptation (Daniel 1:17, 5:11-12)

Number Four: Most dreams require deconstruction.

Some dreams are used to communicate an overall message, but most dreams can be broken down into parts.

	Action	Meaning
1	Record	Write It
2	Recite	Speak It
3	Rehearse	Remember It (dream Book should be a guide for prayer)
4	Reward	Wait For It

Number Five: Identify the main theme, concept, or tone.

Tone	Tense	Type
What feelings are produced by dream	Past, Present or Future	Personal, Observer, Participant

Number Six: Find the OUTCOME or the OBJECTIVE.

What is the ending of the dream?

The Ending	The People	The Places	The Tone

Number Seven: Note any numbers you find or notice.

Numbers carry extreme significance. For example:

Number of people	Number of objects, animals, etc.
Number of episodes, takes, or dreams	The NUMBER OF TIMES the dream occurs.

Number Eight: The more difficult a dream is, the more important it is to life.
Proverbs 25:2: It is the glory of God to conceal a thing: but the honour of kings is to search out a matter.

Number Nine: Ask God questions.
Exercise Time! Ask God five hard questions. These questions will be the basis of your prayer and study life!

Number Ten: Remember that nightmares aren't always demonic.
Don't be in a rush to PANIC. Prayer produced by panic usually affects our accuracy.

Number Eleven: Dreams release divine creativity.
Notice the energy that is created when you tell your dreams. Dreams create atmospheres that sustain creative production.

Guidelines for Dream Navigation

	Things to Think About
1	Don't rush to interpret dreams
2	Allow your rank to develop naturally
3	Read books, but depend on the Holy Spirit
4	Find a circle of dreamers that help push you towards manifestation

Types, Shadows, Models, Patterns, and Templates

Writing Exercise: Write for 2 minutes and then diagnose a tone.

1 Corinthians 14:6: Now, brethren, if I come unto you speaking with tongues, what shall I profit you, except I shall speak to you either by revelation, or by knowledge, or by prophesying, or by doctrine?

List three of your most significant dreams.
What is your interpretation of each dream?
Be sure to pay attention to the most minute of details, leaving no rock unturned.

First Dream

Second Dream

Third Dream

The Office of the Dreamer

Numbers 12:6
And he said, Hear now my words: If there be a prophet among you, I the LORD will make myself known unto him in a vision, and will speak unto him in a dream.

The Realm of Prophetic Places	
Seer	Prophets
Intercessors	Dreamers
Psalmists and Minstrels	

Dreams

Dreams reside in the realm of REVELATION.
When dealing with revelation, we must deal with:

Types	Shadows	Models	Patterns	Templates

Acts 2:17-21
And it shall come to pass in the last days, saith God, I will pour out of my Spirit upon all flesh: and your sons and your daughters shall prophesy, and your young men shall see visions, and your old men shall dream dreams: And on my servants and on my handmaidens I will pour out in those days of my Spirit; and they shall prophesy: And I will shew wonders in heaven above, and signs in the earth beneath; blood, and fire, and vapour of smoke: The sun shall be turned into darkness, and the moon into blood, before that great and notable day of the Lord come: And it shall come to pass, that whosoever shall call on the name of the Lord shall be saved.

Daniel 1:17
As for these four children, God gave them knowledge and skill in all learning and wisdom: and Daniel had understanding in all visions and dreams.

Genesis 20:3
But God came to Abimelech in a dream by night, and said to him, Behold, thou art but a dead man, for the woman which thou hast taken; for she is a man's wife.

The Dimension of Faith

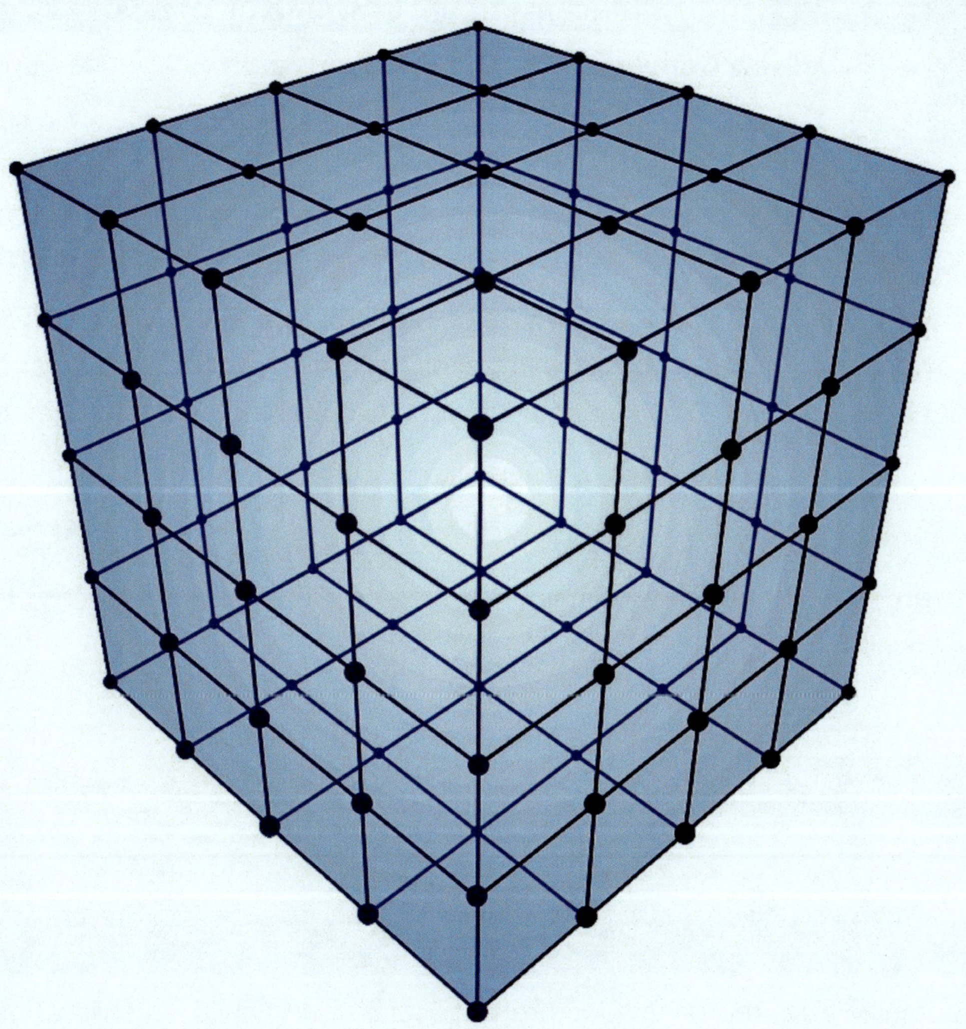

Hebrews 11:1
Now faith is the substance of things hoped for, the evidence of things not seen.

Romans 10:17
So then faith cometh by hearing, and hearing by the word of God.

Three Dimensions of the Word (Reminder)		
Graphe	Logos	Rhema

The Diet of a Believer (Spectrum)			
Stage	**Babe/New Convert**	**Child/ Young Adult**	**Mature Adult**
Diet	Milk	Vegetables/Fruits	Meat

Stage One: Milk

Milk builds bones. It helps the baby to grow taller, stronger and wiser. Milk also helps to build our immune system. Milk represents low-level revelation. All revelation is good and necessary, but for babes, some revelation is too rich, too solid and too earthy for their diets.

Stage Two: Vegetables/Fruits

Vegetables are great for the growing adult! Vegetables are important sources of nutrients! Vegetables and fruits represent healthy revelation that is easier to chew and digest.

There are three levels of this diet. They are:

Cooked	Chopped	Raw/Whole

Cooked
Cooked vegetables/fruits represent food prepared for a young child—a child whose teeth are not strong enough or developed enough to rip through the flesh of raw foods or better yet, raw revelation. This is the stage when the believer is still fully reliant on his or her leaders for Bible study and interpretation. At this stage, the believer has to be forced to eat his/her vegetables. And by forced, I don't mean dominated; it means that a carefully constructed diet has to be developed for the believer, despite the believer's cravings for fast food and junk food.

Chopped		
Chopped vegetables/fruits represent raw food that has either been prepared by a leader/mentor or has been prepared by the child himself. This depends entirely on the maturity level of the believer. So, it goes without saying that within this spectrum, there are three dimensions or levels of this stage; they are:		
Early Childhood	**Adolescence**	**Young Adulthood**
In this phase, the believer still has an appetite for the world that is almost insatiable. Believers who are in this phase are easily offended, emotional, entitled and prideful. For this reason, you will see believers leaving their churches, gossiping about leadership and posting up passive-aggressive statuses on social media about everyone who has offended them. It is for this reason that the believer's diet has to be constructed for him/her. If it is not, they will overindulge themselves in toxicity by watching reality television, listening to music that promotes sexual immorality and violence, and hanging around the wrong people.	In this phase, the believer fluctuates from behaving like a child to behaving like a mature adult. This stage is characterized by rebellion, apologies and then more rebellion. Believers who are in this phase tend to desire a platform more than they desire a pastor. This is because they believe themselves to be mature adults, ready to take on the challenges of the world when, in truth, they are still easily offended, and they lack the depth of revelation needed to lead themselves or others. Believers in this stage can chop their own fruit and prepare some meats.	In this phase, the believer's appetite has changed drastically. The believer now eats whole and raw foods. All the same, the believer doesn't have to be told to eat and what to eat; instead, believers in this phase will study their Bibles on their own, go to church consistently and will even start to volunteer in church. Chopped fruit has to be cut, and as we all know, young children and adolescent children are not mature enough to yield dangerous objects such as knives. This represents teaching. A young adult, on the other hand, is mature enough to lead a small group.

Stage Three: Meat

Meat is for people who have the teeth to chew it and the system to digest it. It's rich with protein, reduces our appetites and it increases our metabolism. This represents revelation that does not have to be broken down for the believer to understand it.

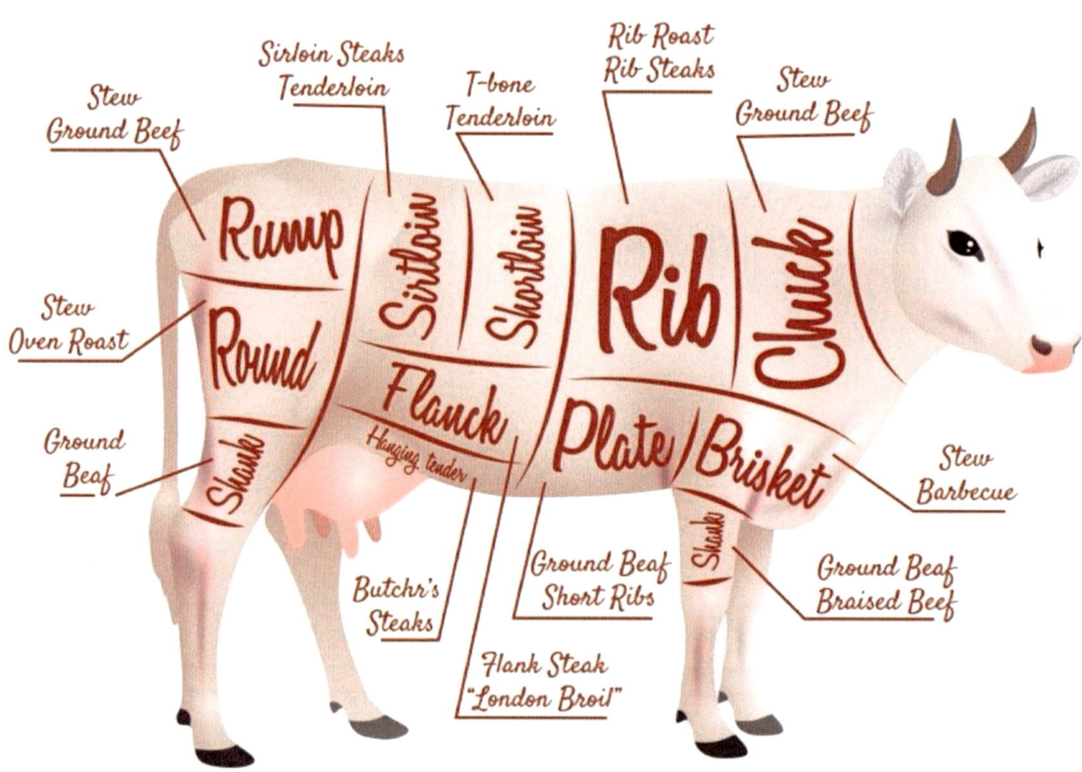
Sirloin Steaks
Tenderloin
Rib Roast
Rib Steaks
T-bone
Tenderloin
Stew
Ground Beef
Stew
Ground Beef
Rump
Sirtloin
Shortloin
Rib
Chuck
Stew
Oven Roast
Round
Flanck
Hanging tender
Plate
Brisket
Ground
Beaf
Shank
Stew
Barbecue
Shank
Ground Beaf
Short Ribs
Ground Beaf
Braised Beef
Butchr's
Steaks
Flank Steak
"London Broil"

How to Grow Your Faith

Faith grows through teaching!
Faith grows through hearing!
Faith grows through conversation!
Faith grows through giving (This directly enlarges your heart)!
Faith grows by opposition!
Faith grows through IMPARTATION!
FAITH GROWS BY EATING!!!!!

The Nose of Faith

According to Cleveland Clinic, the nose has seven functions:

1. **Your nose is the main route for breathing.** The nose and mouth can serve as the pathway of air entering and exiting the lungs. In normal breathing, the nose is the primary pathway. Even with aggressive exercise where mouth breathing becomes dominant, some air continues to pass through the nose. Despite the fact that the mouth is a bigger tube, people feel remarkably uncomfortable if their noses are plugged or congested.
2. **Your nose humidifies the air you breathe.** The nose processes the air we breathe to prepare it for our lungs and throat, which do not tolerate dry air well. As the inhaled air passes through the nose, it is moisturized and humidified, thanks to a complex multiple layer structure called turbinate. Now you know why your throat feels dry when you've been breathing a long time through the mouth: The inhaled air didn't get humidified in the nose.
3. **Your nose cleans the air you breathe.** The air we breathe has all kinds of stuff in it – from oxygen and nitrogen to dust, pollution, allergens, smoke, bacteria, viruses, small bugs and countless other things. The nose helps clean that air. On the surface of the nasal tissues, particularly the turbinate, are cells with small hair-like appendages called cilia that trap much of the bad stuff. Once captured, the bad stuff sits in the mucous and gradually is pushed into the throat, where it's swallowed. Our stomachs tolerate bad stuff much better than our lungs.
4. **Your nose regulates the temperature of the air you breathe.** Just like our throat and lungs do not like dirty air, they do not like air that is too cold or too hot. The passing of the air through the nose allows the air to become more like body temperature, which is

much better tolerated by the tissues. Warming cool air is more common than cooling warm air. That's because humans spend much more of their time in environments below body temperature — 98.6% — than above it. One clear manifestation of the warming and humidifying effect? It's the runny nose we get in cold weather, which is related to condensation of the moisture in the nose when exposed to cold air.

5. **Your nose protects you.** High in the nose are a large number of nerve cells that detect odors. To smell, the air we breathe needs to be pulled high in the nose so that it can come in contact with these nerves. When we have a cold or allergies, it's hard for the air to get to these receptors and so people notice a decreased ability to smell. Smell plays a key role in taste. We have four primary tastes: bitter, sour, sweet and salty. All of the refinements in taste are in fact related to smell. That's why people feel that food is tasteless when their ability to smell is decreased.
6. **Your nose shapes the sound of your voice.** What we hear when people speak and sing is in large part related to the resonating structures of the throat and nose. The voice is produced in the larynx, but that sound is really a buzzing sound. The richness of the sound is determined by how the sound is processed above the larynx, which occurs in the nose and throat. It's the same principle that separates a grand piano from a child's toy piano. The nasal voice we hear in someone with a cold and allergies is due to the loss of this nasal resonation since the air cannot pass through the nose.
7. **Your nose helps you find a mate**. It's amazing how many of our body functions are directed toward sexual activity and reproduction. The nose plays a critical role in our perceptions of sex through the olfactory system. The sense of smell is a key component of how we identify people when we are close to them. The characteristic smell of a person's perfume or cologne or the scent of their shampoo or soap may be important to sexual arousal. The smell of human perspiration has a direct effect on sexual receptors in the brain. Loss of smell correlates with decreased sexual drive.

(Source: ClevelandClinic.org/Health Essentials/7 Surprising Facts About Your Nose/Michael Benninger, MD.)

Of course, the aforementioned article describes the natural functions of the nose, all of which (in spiritual language) denote discernment. Your nose is used for smelling and breathing; one deals with the state of your life, while the other deals with the quality of your life. According to Healthline.com, "The nose is the body's primary organ of smell and also functions as part of the body's respiratory system. Air comes into the body through the nose. As it passes over the specialized cells of the olfactory system, the brain recognizes and identifies smells. Hairs in the nose clean the air of foreign particles." Think of it this way:

1. Your nose will alert you when something is burning; it may even alert you if a dangerous chemical is in your environment. This, of course, can save your life!

2. Your nose will alert you that something you're about to ingest is not palatable for you. If it smells bad to your nose, chances are, you will not like the way it tastes.
3. Anytime a foreign or dangerous particle attempts to enter your body through your nose, your nose hairs will catch most, if not all of the particles, and will respond by causing you to sneeze. This is another extension of deliverance.

So again, the nose deals with your state of life and your quality of life; it has everything to do with discernment. The nose represents the ability to discern or smell a thing. To discern means to differentiate or distinguish between one thing and another; it's your ability to discern between good and evil.

The Mouth of Faith

The mouth has two primary functions; they are eating and speaking. According to WebMD, “The mouth is the beginning of the digestive tract; and, in fact, digestion starts here when taking the first bite of food. Chewing breaks the food into pieces that are more easily digested, while saliva mixes with food to begin the process of breaking it down into a form your body can absorb and use.” It also partners with your nose to aid in breathing, tasting and speaking. You'll notice that if your nose is congested, your voice will sound different. Let's look at a few scriptures.

Romans 10:8-10
But what saith it? The word is nigh thee, even in thy mouth, and in thy heart: that is, the word of faith, which we preach; that if thou shalt confess with thy mouth the Lord Jesus, and shalt believe in thine heart that God hath raised him from the dead, thou shalt be saved. For with the heart man believeth unto righteousness; and with the mouth confession is made unto salvation.

Luke 6:45
A good man out of the good treasure of his heart brings forth good; and an evil man out of the evil treasure of his heart brings forth evil. For out of the abundance of the heart his mouth speaks.

The heart is the belly of the soul. There within lies your belief system; this is where faith is stored. All the same, this is where we store fear. Whatever is found in your heart will be found in your mouth. Jesus said in Matthew 15:11, “Not that which goeth into the mouth defileth a man; but that which cometh out of the mouth, this defileth a man.” What He's dealing with are our confessions. Note: What your mouth doesn't have the maturity to manage, gets stuck in your throat! This directly affects your breathing or, better yet, discernment! Whenever you try to ingest something that's too big, too rich or too tough for your teeth, you will ultimately choke on it. This simply means that you'll be offended by it, unimpressed by it or repulsed by it. In short, what you cannot chew or ingest, you cannot swallow or digest. This means you can't extract the nutrients (revelation) from it. 2 Timothy 4:3-4 (ESV) gives us a picture of what this looks like, “For the time is coming when people will not endure sound teaching, but having itching ears they will accumulate for themselves teachers to suit their own passions, and will turn away from listening to the truth and wander off into myths.”

The Ears of Faith

Romans 10:17
So then faith cometh by hearing, and hearing by the word of God.

According to Healthline.com, “The ears are organs that provide two main functions — hearing and balance — that depend on specialized receptors called hair cells.” Jesus said, “He that hath ears to hear, let him hear.” He wasn't talking about the soft tissue flaps on each side of our heads; He was speaking to believers. In other words, He was addressing those who had faith in Him; what He spoke were the mysteries of the Kingdom of God, all of which could not be discerned by carnal men. For example, consider when Jesus spoke to the crowds in parables. Mark 13:10-13 details this story; it reads, "And the disciples came, and said unto him, Why speakest thou unto them in parables? He answered and said unto them, because it is given unto you to know the mysteries of the kingdom of heaven, but to them it is not given. For whosoever hath, to him shall be given, and he shall have more abundance: but whosoever hath not, from him shall be taken away even that he hath. Therefore, speak I to them in parables: because they seeing see not; and hearing they hear not, neither do they understand." Jesus spoke of high things; that is knowledge that could only be understood by those who were spiritual. He did this so that the people would grow in their faith. Think of it this way. A child sees an apple on a tree, but cannot reach it. The child would then have to get someone who's taller than himself to reach the apple or the child would have to get a ladder or some other apparatus to stand on. The taller person or adult represents the teacher; the ladder or device used represents a platform. If a child uses a platform to reach the apple, there's a big chance that the child will fall or hurt himself, or the child may be not be developed enough to eat the apple. All the same, apples tend to have worms in them, so in short, Jesus was serving as the Teacher to grow them up. Any other way of reaching that revelation would be considered dogmatic and illegal. John 10:1-2 reads, "Verily, verily, I say unto you, He that entereth not by the door into the sheepfold, but climbeth up some other way, the same is a thief and a robber. But he that entereth in by the door is the shepherd of the sheep.

The Hands of Faith

Matthew 9:20-22
And, behold, a woman, which was diseased wlth an issue of blood twelve years, came behind him, and touched the hem of his garment: For she said within herself, If I may but touch his garment, I shall be whole. But Jesus turned him about, and when he saw her, he said, Daughter, be of good comfort; thy faith hath made thee whole. And the woman was made whole from that hour.
Matthew 14:34-36
And when they were gone over, they came into the land of Gennesaret. And when the men of that place had knowledge of him, they sent out into all that country round about, and brought unto him all that were diseased; and besought him that they might only touch the hem of his garment: and as many as touched were made perfectly whole.

According to Physio-pedia.com, "The function of the hand is to grip, grasp and form precise movements, e.g. writing and sewing." The hand lends itself to the faith dynamic because whatever it is that we touch or refuse to touch is a direct reflection of what we believe. For example, Jesus met with two types of people. There were people who had little or small faith;

they insisted on being touched by the Lord or, at minimum, touching His garment. And this is okay! Faith the size of a mustard seed has the ability to move mountains! And then, there were those who had great faith. We see an example of this in Matthew 15:21-28, which reads, “Then Jesus went out from there and departed to the region of Tyre and Sidon. And behold, a woman of Canaan came from that region and cried out to Him, saying, 'Have mercy on me, O Lord, Son of David! My daughter is severely demon-possessed.' But He answered her not a word. And His disciples came and urged Him, saying, 'Send her away, for she cries out after us.' But He answered and said, 'I was not sent except to the lost sheep of the house of Israel.' Then she came and worshiped Him, saying, 'Lord, help me!' But He answered and said, 'It is not good to take the children’s bread and throw it to the little dogs.' And she said, 'Yes, Lord, yet even the little dogs eat the crumbs which fall from their masters’ table.' Then Jesus answered and said to her, 'O woman, great is your faith! Let it be to you as you desire.' And her daughter was healed from that very hour.” Because she had great faith, her daughter was healed without Jesus ever having to touch her.

Additionally, people who have great faith use their hands to express their gifts and creative abilities. It takes a great amount of faith to manifest a book! It takes a great amount of faith to build a business! It takes a great amount of faith to produce an invention! Consider Proverbs 31, which we know has become the single woman's motto. Proverbs 31:10-31 reads, “Who can find a virtuous woman? for her price is far above rubies. The heart of her husband doth safely trust in her, so that he shall have no need of spoil. She will do him good and not evil all the days of her life. She seeketh wool, and flax, and worketh willingly with her hands. She is like the merchants' ships; she bringeth her food from afar. She riseth also while it is yet night, and giveth meat to her household, and a portion to her maidens. She considereth a field, and buyeth it: with the fruit of her hands she planteth a vineyard.

She girdeth her loins with strength, and strengtheneth her arms. She perceiveth that her merchandise is good: her candle goeth not out by night. She layeth her hands to the spindle, and her hands hold the distaff. She stretcheth out her hand to the poor; yea, she reacheth forth her hands to the needy. She is not afraid of the snow for her household: for all her household are clothed with scarlet. She maketh herself coverings of tapestry; her clothing is silk and purple. Her husband is known in the gates, when he sitteth among the elders of the land. She maketh fine linen, and selleth it; and delivereth girdles unto the merchant. Strength and honour are her clothing; and she shall rejoice in time to come. She openeth her mouth with wisdom; and in her tongue is the law of kindness. She looketh well to the ways of her household, and eateth not the bread of idleness. Her children arise up, and call her blessed; her husband also, and he praiseth her. Many daughters have done virtuously, but thou excellest them all. Favour is deceitful, and beauty is vain: but a woman that feareth the LORD, she shall be praised. Give her of the fruit of her hands; and let her own works praise her in the gates."

Notice in the aforementioned scripture, the author deals primarily with the hands of a virtuous woman! This is because faith without works is dead! "Yea, a man may say, thou hast faith, and I have works: shew me thy faith without thy works, and I will shew thee my faith by my works."

The Eyes of Faith

The eye allows us the ability to see; they are a part of our visual system. Often referred to as the "windows of the soul," the eyes allow us to see everything around us and respond to dangerous stimuli within a reasonable space of time. It has everything to do with perspective!

Mark 8:22-26
And he cometh to Bethsaida; and they bring a blind man unto him, and besought him to touch him. And he took the blind man by the hand, and led him out of the town; and when he had spit on his eyes, and put his hands upon him, he asked him if he saw ought. And he looked up, and said, I see men as trees, walking. After that he put his hands again upon his eyes, and made him look up: and he was restored, and saw every man clearly. And he sent him away to his house, saying, neither go into the town, nor tell it to any in the town.

When the blind man was brought to Jesus, he clearly could not see anything. Nevertheless, once his eyes were opened, his perspective was still warped. This had everything to do with his faith. You see, when Jesus touches someone for the first time, His goal is to build that person's faith; this way, He can perform even greater miracles. The size of your miracle is in direct proportion to the size of your faith! The man received a small miracle initially, but once he realized that he could see, his faith increased. From there, Jesus was able to fully restore his sight!

All too often, believers get wounded and even traumatized because of the events they've had to endure. This is why many people receive small miracles when they approach the altar of their local churches. Because of their experiences with toxic people, most broken individuals approach prayer and deliverance with trust issues. Consequently, they get a small measure of freedom, but this is great! It is oftentimes notable enough to increase their trust in man and faith in God, thereby, allowing God to perform an even greater miracle. Again, this has everything to do with perspective!

The Power of Faith

Luke 17:5-10
The apostles said to the Lord, "Increase our faith!" And the Lord answered, "If you have faith the size of a mustard seed, you can say to this mulberry tree, 'Be uprooted and planted in the sea,' and it will obey you.'"

If we are going to change the world, we need grown man faith. This is the purpose of the five-fold ministry; that is, to mature the body of Christ in measure, stature and fullness. Ephesians

4:11-15 says it this way, “And he gave some, apostles; and some, prophets; and some, evangelists; and some, pastors and teachers; for the perfecting of the saints, for the work of the ministry, for the edifying of the body of Christ: Till we all come in the unity of the faith, and of the knowledge of the Son of God, unto a perfect man, unto the measure of the stature of the fulness of Christ: That we henceforth be no more children, tossed to and fro, and carried about with every wind of doctrine, by the sleight of men, and cunning craftiness, whereby they lie in wait to deceive; but speaking the truth in love, may grow up into him in all things, which is the head, even Christ.”

Power is comprised of three elements:

1. **Potential:** This is the seed or the capability for someone or something to tangibly, audibly, morally, physically and or spiritually effect change.
2. **Faith:** This is the substance of whatever it is that is hoped for, coupled with the evidence of things unseen. What this means is that it is more than just a belief, it is the empowerment of that belief through planning and action. Think of it this way—if you were driving down a busy freeway and you wanted to change lanes, the only way you'd do so is if you believed that you had both space and opportunity to safely make the transition. This is how faith works. Even though you don't necessarily know without a shadow of doubt that you'd make the transition safely, you have faith in your own abilities, so you'd likely zoom over into the next lane. Believing you could safely transition over is nothing; you'd stay in the other lane until you took action. So, faith is belief plus action.
3. **Works:** This is the action or the substance of faith. This is when you use your own personal resources, whether it be your physical strength, your time, your money or whatever resources you have to carry out an action. Notice in the aforementioned scripture, Jesus said to His disciples that if they had faith the size of a mustard seed AND they spoke to the mulberry tree, it would have to obey them. In this, they had to use their voices, and not just that, they had to back their command up with their faith; that is, the belief that the mulberry tree had to obey them.

Faith has power, but it must first be plugged in and utilized for that power to be extracted. Think about the story of Elijah and the widow. Let's look at a couple of scriptures.

1 Kings 17:2-8
And the word of the LORD came unto him, saying, get thee hence, and turn thee eastward, and hide thyself by the brook Cherith, that is before Jordan. And it shall be, that thou shalt drink of the brook; and I have commanded the ravens to feed thee there. So he went and did

according unto the word of the LORD: for he went and dwelt by the brook Cherith, that is before Jordan. And the ravens brought him bread and flesh in the morning, and bread and flesh in the evening; and he drank of the brook. And it came to pass after a while, that the brook dried up, because there had been no rain in the land. And the word of the LORD came unto him, saying, Arise, get thee to Zarephath, which belongeth to Zidon, and dwell there: behold, I have commanded a widow woman there to sustain thee.

1 Kings 17:10-16
So he arose and went to Zarephath. And when he came to the gate of the city, behold, the widow woman was there gathering of sticks: and he called to her, and said, Fetch me, I pray thee, a little water in a vessel, that I may drink. And as she was going to fetch it, he called to her, and said, bring me, I pray thee, a morsel of bread in thine hand. And she said, As the LORD thy God liveth, I have not a cake, but an handful of meal in a barrel, and a little oil in a cruse: and, behold, I am gathering two sticks, that I may go in and dress it for me and my son, that we may eat it, and die. And Elijah said unto her, Fear not; go and do as thou hast said: but make me thereof a little cake first, and bring it unto me, and after make for thee and for thy son. For thus saith the LORD God of Israel, The barrel of meal shall not waste, neither shall the cruse of oil fail, until the day that the LORD sendeth rain upon the earth. And she went and did according to the saying of Elijah: and she, and he, and her house, did eat many days. And the barrel of meal wasted not, neither did the cruse of oil fail, according to the word of the LORD, which he spake by Elijah.

POTENTIAL IS POWER IN THE WOMB

The widow had potential. The widow had faith. The works was the last ingredient needed to extract that potential and turn it into power. And hear me—she had been given a hard charge! Elijah literally asked her to give him her and her son's last meal! Most people would have gotten offended, but God said that He'd already commanded her to feed Elijah. Did she hear God's audible voice? Probably not. She felt inspiration! The more Elijah spoke to her, the more her faith was charged. You see, the scriptures tell us that God had commanded the ravens to feed Elijah at the brook. What this tells us is that Elijah had tapped into divine provision, so whether or not the widow woman obeyed God was of no detriment to him. Had she been disobedient, God would have raised up someone or something else to ensure that Elijah would eat. When she obeyed God, she tapped into the supernatural provision that God had allotted to Elijah. This is why Matthew 10:41 states, “He that receiveth a prophet in the name of a prophet shall receive a prophet's reward; and he that receiveth a righteous man in the name of a righteous man shall receive a righteous man's reward."

Faith has the ability to make the impossible possible; it is the supernatural ability to provoke Heaven to move in the Earth through knowledge of the Word and the application of the Word. It is marrying the "super" to the "natural" to create the supernatural. Remember, God is Supreme, meaning, He is superior to everything and everyone. We, on the other hand, are natural. When the Supreme God touches the natural world, the supernatural occurs.

Levels of Faith

1	Every level has an entrance and an exit.	6	Every level has assignments.
2	Every level has an expiration date.	7	Every level has gifts.
3	Every level has resources.	8	Every level has anointing.
4	Every level has tests.	9	Every level has rank.
5	Every level has laws.	10	Every level has speed.

John 3:34

For he whom God hath sent speaketh the words of God: for God giveth not the Spirit by measure unto him.

The word "measure" in the aforementioned scripture deals with a dimension of faith. Let's look at the three waves of faith.

Measure of Faith	Surrogate Faith	Saving Faith

Measure of Faith

Romans 12:7

Having then gifts differing according to the grace that is given to us, whether prophecy, let us prophesy according to the proportion of faith.

Surrogate Faith

This is the faith of someone else, for example, the faith of your mother or grandmother.

Psalm 106:23
Therefore he said that he would destroy them, had not Moses his chosen stood before him in the breach, to turn away his wrath, lest he should destroy them.

Saving Faith
Romans 10:9
That if thou shalt confess with thy mouth the Lord Jesus, and shalt believe in thine heart that God hath raised him from the dead, thou shalt be saved.

Dimensions of Faith

Little Faith	Strong Faith	Great Faith
"Fearful, displaying a lack of total trust; was used by the Lord as a tender rebuke for anxiety and fear." (Vine's Complete Expository Dictionary) "If God so clothes the grass of the field, which today is, and tomorrow is thrown into the oven, will He not much more clothe you, O you of little faith?" (Matthew 6:30) "But He said to them, 'Why are you fearful, O you of little faith?' Then He arose and rebuked the winds and the sea, and there was a great calm. (Matthew 8:26)	He staggered not at the promise of God through unbelief; but was strong in faith, giving glory to God." (Romans 4:20) Abraham had a faith that refused to surrender or be defeated. Following the faith of Abraham is the way to receive what might be considered impossible and unprecedented.	An unrelenting, totally persuaded type of faith, that does not give up until the request is granted. A Centurion who had asked Jesus to heal his sick child, and whose faith was so great that he said, "Lord, I am not worthy that You should come under my roof. But only speak a word, and my servant will be healed." "When Jesus heard it, He marveled, and said to those who followed, "Assuredly, I say to you, I have not found such great faith, not even in Israel!" (Matthew 8:8-10) And there was the woman from Canaan, a Gentile, (not a Jew). The Gentiles as a rule, had very little, if any faith in God. This woman requested Jesus to heal her severely demon-possessed daughter. When

Little Faith	Strong Faith	Great Faith
		Jesus refused, saying that He had only been sent to the Jews, she persisted, and demonstrated a faith so great that it brought the following response from Jesus: "...O woman, great is your faith! Let it be to you as you desire..." (Matthew 15:21-28)

Degrees of Faith

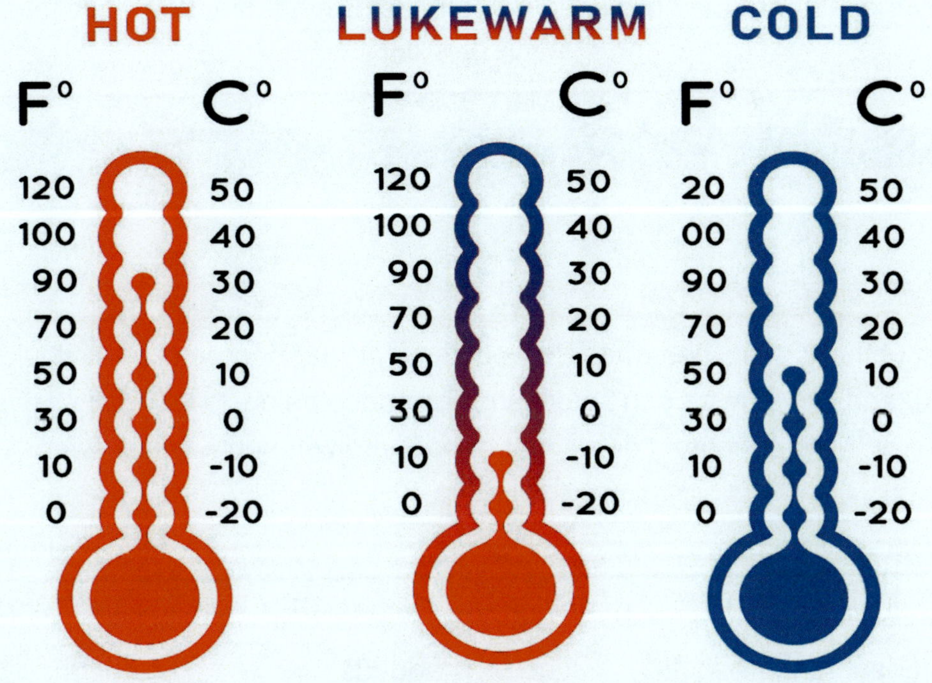

Faith without Works
"But someone will say, 'You have faith, and I have works.' Show me your faith without your works, and I will show you my faith by my works." (James 2:18)
A faith without works passively believes and accepts the Bible literally, but without action. Many people believe and have faith that God can do all His Word says. They believe in miracles, yet fail to act on His Word.

Faith without Root
"...the ones on the rock are those who, when they hear, receive the word with joy; and these have no root, who believe for a while and in time of temptation fall away." (Luke 8:13)
Jesus spoke of having faith without root. It is the kind that springs up quickly, and beautifully, but because it has no depth, fails just as quickly when temptation and trials come along. For the most part this is because the soil has not been properly prepared by digging and searching for knowledge, guidance, and truth, in God's Word.

Faith and Unbelief
Jesus said unto him, If thou canst believe, all things are possible to him that believeth. And straightway the father of the child cried out, and said with tears, Lord, I believe; help thou mine unbelief. (Mark 9:23-24)
Sometimes, faith and unbelief coexist.

Challenge

Below is a list of the 12 Apostles who followed Jesus. What degree of faith would you say that each man had, and why? If you don't have enough space below to list your answer, please use a Word document or a sheet of paper to write out your answer.

Peter	James	John
Andrew	Bartholomew (Nathaniel)	James, the Lesser (Younger)
Judas	Jude of Thaddeus	Matthew (Levi)
Philip	Simon, the Zealot	Thomas

Your Answer

Your Answer

Levels of Thinking

Thinker	Level
Non-Thinker	Low Level
Over Thinker	Low Level
Narrow Thinker	Low Level
Open Thinker	Low Level
The Imaginator	High Level
The Dream Level	High Level
The Visionary	High Level
Mega Thinker/Mega Mind (Strategic Thinker)	High Level

Bloom's Taxonomy of Thinking Skills

When working with special needs students, it is helpful to recognize certain attributes about the kind of learning tasks we are giving children to do. We typically assign reading, followed by some discussion, and end up with some form of evaluation. Let me suggest a "model" that more closely reflects information about how we all organize information and ideas.

Many years ago, Dr. Benjamin Bloom proposed a theoretical ranking of the levels of thinking that people use. At the simple and basic level, Bloom suggested, people operate at a very "concrete" level of knowledge. Moving beyond that, people are able to "comprehend" what the facts are about and to some extent, they are able to manipulate those ideas by comparing or contrasting or even retelling events in their own words.

At the next level of complexity of thought, individuals are able to "apply" what they have learned from facts and comprehension. This level of thinking permits them to demonstrate knowledge, solve or apply what they know to new and related situations. Moving beyond "application," the next level of thinking allows people to "analyze" what they know. At this level, typically they can classify, categorize, discriminate or detect information.

The two highest levels of cognitive thought, according to Bloom, are synthesis and evaluation. In "synthesis," the individual is able to put ideas together, propose plans, form solutions, and create new information. In the "evaluation" stage, the thinker is able to make choices, select, evaluate and make judgments about information and situations.

Bloom's Taxonomy

Definition: Bloom's taxonomy, taxonomy of educational objectives, developed in the 1950s by the American educational psychologist Benjamin Bloom, which fostered a common vocabulary for thinking about learning goals. Bloom's taxonomy engendered a way to align educational goals, curricula, and assessments that are used in schools, and it structured the breadth and depth of the instructional activities and curriculum that teachers provide for students. Few educational theorists or researchers have had as profound an impact on American educational practice as Bloom.
(Source: Encyclopedia Britannica)

From Most Concrete to Most Abstract Levels

	Levels	Description
1	**Knowledge**	Recall of something encountered before, but without having to change it, use it or understand it; facts.
2	**Comprehension**	Understanding the knowledge that has been acquired without needing to relate it to other information.
3	**Application**	Use of a learned concept to resolve some situation or solve a new problem in an appropriate way.
4	**Analysis**	Taking something learned apart into separate components for purposes of thinking about the parts and how they fit together.
5	**Synthesis**	Generating or creating something different by assembling or connecting ideas in a way that makes a whole.
6	**Evaluation**	Looking at the particular value of materials, information or methods in characterizing the whole.

Sola Scriptura

The words “Sola Scriptura” mean “Bible alone.” Sola Scriptura is a Protestant doctrine which simply means that the scriptures ALONE are the primary source for ALL biblical doctrine. It asserts that the scriptures are revelation shared with us directly from YAHWEH, which makes them the COMPLETE and ABSOLUTE authority of all things, including the church. Sola Scriptura upholds the divinity of the scriptures, while emphasizing the fallibility of man and the divisibility of man-made traditions and doctrines.

Theopedia.com defines it this way, “Scripture alone (from the Reformation slogan Sola Scriptura) is the teaching that scripture is the Church's only infallible and sufficient rule for deciding issues of faith and practices that involve doctrines. While the Bible does not contain all knowledge, it does contain that which is necessary for salvation. Indeed, if something is not found in Scripture, it is not binding upon the believer. This view does not deny that the Church has the authority to teach God's Word. Furthermore, while tradition is valuable, it but must be tested by the higher authority of the Scriptures. Sola Scriptura does not mean that the Reformers rejected everything that every Christian in earlier ages have said: indeed, they often cited the early Christians as supporters of their own positions. However, they recognized that those earlier believers were not inspired, were not inerrant, and, in fact, quite often made errors in their judgments and beliefs, just as people do today. The only infallible rule of faith, they argued, is found in the pages of Holy Writ.”

In short, Sola Scriptura places weight on the infallible Word of God. Why is this important? Because the Roman Catholic Church used to hold absolute power over the law of the land in Rome, and the church had bishops called magisterium. They were rendered to be the “true interpreters of scriptures,” meaning, the country was subject, not to the Word, but to the Pope and the magisterium's interpretation of the scriptures. Because of this, the magisterium could not be challenged. The problem with this was that humans are fallible, meaning, they are subject to error, plus, men and women having absolute rule had already proven to be a detriment to any given kingdom. King Henry VIII was a prime example of this. He was the king of England from 1509 until 1547. During that time, the Church of England (the Roman Catholic Church) was the sole authority over England. Even the king himself was subject to the laws of the church. The Pope had full papal supremacy. According to Lumen Learning, “Papal supremacy is the doctrine of the Roman Catholic Church that the pope, by reason of his office as Vicar of Christ and as pastor of the entire Christian Church, has full, supreme, and universal power over the whole church, a power which he can always exercise unhindered—that, in brief, 'the Pope enjoys, by divine institution, supreme, full, immediate, and universal power in the care of souls'” (Source: Lumin Learning/ER Services/The Development of Papal Supremacy). King Henry VIII wanted to annul his marriage to his wife, Catherine of Aragon, because of his infatuation with a woman by the name of Anne Boelyn. Nevertheless, Pope Clement would not permit him to divorce his wife and marry Ms. Boelyn. Incensed by the pope's refusal to grant him the annulment, King Henry VIII launched a political war called the English Reformation, where he fought to separate the Church from papal authority. Of course, he was successful in his endeavors, and he went on to divorce his wife, Catherine of Aragon, and he then proceeded to marry his love interest, Anne Boelyn. Let's look at a timeline of his marriages.

Wife of King Henry VIII	Fate	Reason
Catherine of Aragon	**Divorced**	She failed to produce a male heir for the king.
Anne Boelyn	**Executed**	She gave birth to a daughter, but miscarried their second child. Because of this, King Henry VIII accused her of adultery, incest and witchcraft. Consequently, he had her beheaded.
Jane Seymour	**Died**	Jane Seymour successfully gave the king a son, but died 12 days later of blood poisoning.
Anne of Cleves	**Divorced**	Their marriage was strictly political. The king married Anne to form a political alliance between England and the Protestant princes of Germany. Six months later, King Henry decided that the political alliance was no longer beneficial to him, so he divorced Anne of Cleves.
Catherine Howard	**Executed**	King Henry accused this particular wife of treason, claiming that she'd committed adultery. He then had her beheaded for her alleged crime.
Katherine Parr	**Survived**	King Henry's sixth and final wife actually outlived him!

While we do not ascribe to Catholic doctrine, the truth of the matter is that King Henry VIII wasn't necessarily fighting against the Pope, he was fighting against the Word. What he decided to do was place the Church under his authority through a policy called the Divine Rights of Kings. In short, this doctrine asserted that kings had been divinely appointed by God, and as such, could not fall under the earthly authority of a human being. In other words, the monarch would not have to be accountable to anyone! And hear me—this wasn't the first time that an event like this had taken place! Before the Bible was written out in text, many kings in the biblical era attempted to usurp God's power by placing their desires over the words and warnings of the prophets. Let's look at a timeline of some of Israel's kings!

King/Ruler	Scripture
Jehoahaz Evil	**2 Kings 13:1-2:** In the three and twentieth year of Joash the son of Ahaziah king of Judah Jehoahaz the son of Jehu began to reign over Israel in Samaria, and reigned seventeen years. And he did that which was evil in the sight of the LORD, and followed the sins of Jeroboam the son of Nebat, which made Israel to sin; he departed not therefrom.
Jehoash Evil	**2 Kings 13:10-11:** In the thirty and seventh year of Joash king of Judah began Jehoash the son of Jehoahaz to reign over Israel in Samaria, and reigned sixteen years. And he did that which was evil in the sight of the LORD; he departed not from all the sins of Jeroboam the son of Nebat, who made Israel sin: but he walked therein.
Jeroboam II Evil	**2 Kings 14:23-24:** In the fifteenth year of Amaziah the son of Joash king of Judah Jeroboam the son of Joash king of Israel began to reign in Samaria, and reigned forty and one years. And he did that which was evil in the sight of the LORD: he departed not from all the sins of Jeroboam the son of Nebat, who made Israel to sin.
Zachariah Evil	**2 Kings 15:8-9:** In the thirty and eighth year of Azariah king of Judah did Zachariah the son of Jeroboam reign over Israel in Samaria six months. And he did that which was evil in the sight of the LORD, as his fathers had done: he departed not from the sins of Jeroboam the son of Nebat, who made Israel to sin.
Shallum N/A	**2 Kings 15:13-15:** Shallum the son of Jabesh began to reign in the nine and thirtieth year of Uzziah king of Judah; and he reigned a full month in Samaria. For Menahem the son of Gadi went up from Tirzah, and came to Samaria, and smote Shallum the son of Jabesh in Samaria, and slew him, and reigned in his stead. And the rest of the acts of Shallum, and his conspiracy which he made,

King/Ruler	Scripture
	behold, they are written in the book of the chronicles of the kings of Israel.
Menahem **Evil**	**2 Kings 15:17-18:** In the nine and thirtieth year of Azariah king of Judah began Menahem the son of Gadi to reign over Israel, and reigned ten years in Samaria. And he did that which was evil in the sight of the LORD: he departed not all his days from the sins of Jeroboam the son of Nebat, who made Israel to sin.
Pekahiah **Evil**	**2 Kings 15:23-24:** In the fiftieth year of Azariah king of Judah Pekahiah the son of Menahem began to reign over Israel in Samaria, and reigned two years. And he did that which was evil in the sight of the LORD: he departed not from the sins of Jeroboam the son of Nebat, who made Israel to sin.
Pekah **Evil**	**2 Kings 15:27-28:** In the two and fiftieth year of Azariah king of Judah Pekah the son of Remaliah began to reign over Israel in Samaria, and reigned twenty years. And he did that which was evil in the sight of the LORD: he departed not from the sins of Jeroboam the son of Nebat, who made Israel to sin.
Hoshea **Evil**	**2 Kings 17:1-2:** In the twelfth year of Ahaz king of Judah began Hoshea the son of Elah to reign in Samaria over Israel nine years. And he did that which was evil in the sight of the LORD, but not as the kings of Israel that were before him.

Let's look at the most famous example to date! Ahab!

1 Kings 16:30-33
And Ahab the son of Omri did evil in the sight of the LORD above all that *were* before him. And it came to pass, as if it had been a light thing for him to walk in the sins of Jeroboam the son of Nebat, that he took to wife Jezebel the daughter of Ethbaal king of the Zidonians, and went and served Baal, and worshipped him. And he reared up an altar for Baal in the house of Baal, which he had built in Samaria. And Ahab made a grove; and Ahab did more to provoke the LORD God of Israel to anger than all the kings of Israel that were before him.

Ahab had at least five encounters with God's prophets!

Prophet	Scripture
Elijah	1 Kings 17:1
Unnamed Prophet	1 Kings 20:22
Unnamed Prophet	1 Kings 20:34-43
Elijah	1 Kings 21:1-16
Micaiah	1 Kings 22

The number five, biblically speaking, represents grace. God extended His grace to Ahab repeatedly, but he would not wholeheartedly repent for him and his wife's witchcraft and rebellion. They took Jezebel's doctrines and deities, and attempted to make them supreme over God's people. They killed off many of God's prophets, stole land from Naboth and committed blasphemy. This is why it is absolutely dangerous for a human being to have absolute power with no accountability! Someone has to hold a leader accountable to the Word of God, and of course, the prophets attempted to do this with Ahab, but he refused to submit to their counsel.

Sola Scriptura simply disallowed the scriptures from becoming subject to man's interpretation and man's abuse of them. The Pope was right about the king not having the legal standing (biblically speaking) to divorce his wife, but he was wrong (morally speaking) in interfering with another human's decisions. God allows us to freely exercise the dominion He's given us, and what we do with it will determine who and what we fall subject to! All the same, King Henry VIII abused this power once it was granted to him. He proved once and for all why a mere human cannot and should not have absolute authority over anything; we all need accountability!

The second aspect of Sola Scriptura was the sufficiency of scripture. Again, the Catholic Church believed that the scriptures needed to be supplemented with extra-biblical rituals and beliefs, many of which were pagan in origin. And while Reformers agreed that God can and does speak extra-biblically, they argued that the Bible is sufficient for salvation. In other words, Sola Scriptura was not established to discredit science or the allegorical interpretations of the Bible; it simply deems the Word (as it is written) as the supreme authority! This is to counter man's consistent attempts to make the scriptures subject to his opinions, lusts and emotions.

Challenge

Which of the following quotes are NOT in the Bible?

Do not quench the Spirit.	The Lord works in mysterious ways.
Cleanliness is next to Godliness.	I and My Father are one.
Jesus Christ is the same yesterday and today and forever.	Do unto others as you would have them do unto you.
Jesus wept.	Money is the root of all evil.
God helps those who help themselves.	The Lord bless you and keep you.

List ten more extra-biblical sayings that most believers think are in the Bible.

1	
2	
3	
4	
5	
6	
7	
8	
9	
10	

Holy Spirit Symbolism

The following descriptions was taken from CatholicCulture.org:

Water

The symbolism of water signifies the Holy Spirit's action in Baptism, since after the invocation of the Holy Spirit it becomes the efficacious sacramental sign of new birth: just as the gestation of our first birth took place in water, so the water of Baptism truly signifies that our birth into the divine life is given to us in the Holy Spirit. As "by one Spirit we were all baptized," so we are also "made to drink of one Spirit." Thus the Spirit is also personally the living water welling up from Christ crucified as its source and welling up in us to eternal life.

Anointing

The symbolism of anointing with oil also signifies the Holy Spirit, to the point of becoming a synonym for the Holy Spirit. In Christian initiation, anointing is the sacramental sign of Confirmation, called "chrismation" in the Churches of the East. Its full force can be grasped only in relation to the primary anointing accomplished by the Holy Spirit, that of Jesus. Christ (in Hebrew "messiah") means the one "anointed" by God's Spirit. There were several anointed ones of the Lord in the Old Covenant, pre-eminently King David. But Jesus is God's Anointed in a unique way: the humanity the Son assumed was entirely anointed by the Holy Spirit. the Holy Spirit established him as "Christ."

The Virgin Mary conceived Christ by the Holy Spirit who, through the angel, proclaimed Him the Christ at His birth, and prompted Simeon to come to the temple to see Him. The Spirit filled Christ and the power of the Spirit went out from Him in His acts of healing and of saving. Finally, it was the Spirit who raised Jesus from the dead. Now, fully established as "Christ" in His humanity and victorious over death, Jesus pours out the Holy Spirit abundantly until "the saints" constitute - in their union with the humanity of the Son of God - that perfect man "to the measure of the stature of the fullness of Christ": "the whole Christ," in St. Augustine's expression.

Fire

While water signifies birth and the fruitfulness of life given in the Holy Spirit, fire symbolizes the transforming energy of the Holy Spirit's actions. the prayer of the prophet Elijah, who "arose like fire" and whose "word burned like a torch," brought down fire from heaven on the sacrifice on Mount Carmel. This event was a "figure" of the fire of the Holy Spirit, who transforms what he touches. John the Baptist, who goes "before [the Lord] in the spirit and power of Elijah," proclaims Christ as the one who "will baptize you with the Holy Spirit and with fire." Jesus will say of the Spirit: "I came to cast fire upon the earth; and would that it were already kindled!" In the form of tongues "as of fire," the Holy Spirit rests on the disciples on the morning of Pentecost and fills them with himself The spiritual tradition has retained this symbolism of fire as one of the most expressive images of the Holy Spirit's actions. "Do not quench the Spirit."

Cloud and Light

These two images occur together in the manifestations of the Holy Spirit. In the theophanies of the Old Testament, the cloud, now obscure, now luminous, reveals the living and saving God, while veiling the transcendence of his glory - with Moses on Mount Sinai, at the tent of meeting, and during the wandering in the desert, and with Solomon at the dedication of the Temple. In the Holy Spirit, Christ fulfills these figures. the Spirit comes upon the Virgin Mary and "overshadows" her, so that she might conceive and give birth to Jesus. On the mountain of Transfiguration, the Spirit in the "cloud came and overshadowed" Jesus, Moses and Elijah, Peter, James and John, and "a voice came out of the cloud, saying, 'This is my Son, my Chosen; listen to him!'" Finally, the cloud took Jesus out of the sight of the disciples on the day of his ascension and will reveal him as Son of man in glory on the day of his final coming.

The Seal

The seal is a symbol close to that of anointing. "The Father has set his seal" on Christ and also seals us in him. Because this seal indicates the indelible effect of the anointing with the Holy Spirit in the sacraments of Baptism, Confirmation, and Holy Orders, the image of the seal (sphragis) has been used in some theological traditions to express the indelible "character" imprinted by these three unrepeatable sacraments.

The Hand

Jesus heals the sick and blesses little children by laying hands on them. In his name the apostles will do the same. Even more pointedly, it is by the Apostles' imposition of hands that the Holy Spirit is given. The Letter to the Hebrews lists the imposition of hands among the "fundamental elements" of its teaching. The Church has kept this sign of the all-powerful outpouring of the Holy Spirit in its sacramental epiclesis.

The Finger

"It is by the finger of God that [Jesus] cast out demons." If God's law was written on tablets of stone "by the finger of God," then the "letter from Christ" entrusted to the care of the apostles, is written "with the Spirit of the living God, not on tablets of stone, but on tablets of human hearts." The hymn Veni Creator Spiritus invokes the Holy Spirit as the "finger of the Father's right hand."

The Dove

At the end of the flood, whose symbolism refers to Baptism, a dove released by Noah returns with a fresh olive-tree branch in its beak as a sign that the earth was again habitable. When Christ comes up from the water of his baptism, the Holy Spirit, in the form of a dove, comes down upon him and remains with him. The Spirit comes down and remains in the purified hearts of the baptized. In certain churches, the Eucharist is reserved in a metal receptacle in the form of a dove (columbarium) suspended above the altar. Christian iconography traditionally uses a dove to suggest the Spirit.

(Source: CatholicCulture.org/Catechism of the Catholic Church/Symbols of the Holy Spirit)

The Names of the Holy Spirit

The following was taken from GotQuestions.com:

Author of Scripture: (2 Peter 1:21; 2 Timothy 3:16) The Bible is inspired, literally "God-breathed," by the Holy Spirit, the third Person of the Trinity. The Spirit moved the authors of all 66 books to record exactly what He breathed into their hearts and minds. As a ship is moved through the water by wind in its sails, so the biblical writers were borne along by the Spirit's impulse.

Comforter / Counselor / Advocate: (Isaiah 11:2; John 14:16; 15:26; 16:7) All three words are translations of the Greek *parakletos*, from which we get "Paraclete," another name for the Spirit. When Jesus went away, His disciples were greatly distressed because they had lost His comforting presence. But He promised to send the Spirit to comfort, console, and guide those who belong to Christ. The Spirit also "bears witness" with our spirits that we belong to Him and thereby assures us of salvation.

Convicter of Sin: (John 16:7-11) The Spirit applies the truths of God to men's own minds in order to convince them by fair and sufficient arguments that they are sinners. He does this through the conviction in our hearts that we are not worthy to stand before a holy God, that we need His righteousness, and that judgment is certain and will come to all men one day. Those who deny these truths rebel against the conviction of the Spirit.

Deposit / Seal / Earnest: (2 Corinthians 1:22; 5:5; Ephesians 1:13-14) The Holy Spirit is God's seal on His people, His claim on us as His very own. The gift of the Spirit to believers is a down payment on our heavenly inheritance, which Christ has promised us and secured for us at the cross. It is because the Spirit has sealed us that we are assured of our salvation. No one can break the seal of God.

Guide: (John 16:13) Just as the Spirit guided the writers of Scripture to record truth, so does He promise to guide believers to know and understand that truth. God's truth is "foolishness" to the world, because it is "spiritually discerned" (1 Corinthians 2:14). Those who belong to Christ have the indwelling Spirit who guides us into all we need to know in regard to spiritual matters. Those who do not belong to Christ have no "interpreter" to guide them to know and understand God's Word.

Indweller of Believers: (Romans 8:9-11; Ephesians 2:21-22; 1 Corinthians 6:19) The Holy Spirit resides in the hearts of God's people, and that indwelling is the distinguishing characteristic of the regenerated person. From within believers, He directs, guides, comforts, and influences us, as well as producing in us the fruit of the Spirit (Galatians 5:22-23). He provides the intimate connection between God and His children. All true believers in Christ have the Spirit residing in their hearts.

(Source: GotQuestions.org/What are the Names and Titles of the Holy Spirit?)

The Functions of the Holy Spirit

Functions	Scripture
Dwell in us	John 14:17
Teach us all things	John 14:26
Bring Jesus' words to remembrance	John 14:26
Testify of Jesus	John 15:26
Reprove the world of sin, righteousness and judgment	John 16:8
Guide us in all truth	John 16:13
Show (tell) us things that are to come	John 16:13-15
Glorify the Lord, Jesus Christ	John 16:14

Ten Plagues of Egypt

What is a plague? According to Merriam Webster, it is a disastrous evil or affliction.

The Greek word for "plague" is "plégé", and it literally means a blow, an affliction, a stripe or a wound. Plagues were oftentimes the result of God responding to the sins of mankind. The overall objective wasn't to punish man for his incessant need to sin, but to get him to repent. And while this was oftentimes effective, it was short-lived. And as we all know, the Israelites were held in captivity in Egypt for well over four-hundred years. As God set the stage for their deliverance, He had Moses to stand in as an intercessor and prophet, speaking on behalf of Him to Pharaoh. Of course, the scriptures tell us that God hardened Pharaoh's heart; this was so that He could glorify His name and build the faith of the Israelites.

Below, you will find the ten plagues that God brought upon Egypt. Be sure to memorize these so that you can study and come to understand the patterns of God.

Plague	Scripture
Water to Blood	Exodus 7:14–24
Frogs	Exodus 7:25–8:15
Lice	Exodus 8:16–8:19
Flies	Exodus 8:20-32
Pestilence of Livestock	Exodus 9:1-7
Plague of Boils	Exodus 9:8-12
Hail	Exodus 9:13-35
Locusts	Exodus 10:1-20
Darkness for Three Days	Exodus 10:21-29
Death of Firstborn	Exodus 11 and 12

plague (n.)

late 14c., plage, "affliction, calamity, evil, scourge, severe trouble or vexation;" early 15c., "malignant disease," from Old French plage (14c., Modern French plaie), from Late Latin plaga "affliction; slaughter, destruction," used in Vulgate for "pestilence," from Latin plaga "stroke, wound," probably from root of plangere "to strike, lament (by beating the breast)," from or cognate with Greek (Doric) plaga "blow," from PIE root *plak- (2) "to strike."

Sometimes in Middle English also "a strike a blow" (late 14c.). The Latin word also is the source of Old Irish plag (genitive plaige) "plague, pestilence," German Plage, Dutch plaage. Meaning "epidemic that causes many deaths" is from 1540s; specifically in reference to bubonic plague from c. 1600. Modern spelling follows French, which had plague from 15c. Weakened sense of "anything annoying" is from c. 1600.

Source: www.etymonline.com/word/plague

Synonyms for Strike				
Beat	Afflict	Force	Pummel	Affect
Reach	Inspire	Devastate	Collide	Touch
Chastise	Thrust	Buffet	Drive	Punish

When Eli's Eyes Grow Dim

1 Samuel 2:22-25
Now Eli was very old, and heard all that his sons did unto all Israel; and how they lay with the women that assembled at the door of the tabernacle of the congregation. And he said unto them, why do ye such things? For I hear of your evil dealings by all this people. Nay, my sons; for it is no good report that I hear: ye make the LORD'S people to transgress. If one man sin against another, the judge shall judge him: but if a man sin against the LORD, who shall intreat for him? Notwithstanding they hearkened not unto the voice of their father, because the LORD would slay them.

1 Samuel 3:2
And it came to pass at that time, when Eli was laid down in his place, and his eyes began to wax dim, that he could not see.

Deuteronomy 34:7
Moses *was* one hundred and twenty years old when he died. His eyes were not dim nor his natural vigor diminished.

The Kingdom of God, in every given generation, progresses at the rate of that generation's revelation, understanding of God and perception of God. For example, let's juxtapose Moses with Eli. Eli's eyes got dim, but the scriptures tell us that Moses' eyes never got dim. In other words, revelation should not fade with old age. As a matter of fact, it should get brighter; it should get clearer! When the author talks about Eli's eyes, he's not just talking about his physical eyes, he was also dealing with his spiritual senses or, better yet, spiritual sight. A lot of times when we think about spiritual sight, we think about discernment, but discernment is actually a faculty of the nose. It deals with our ability to smell in the spirit, but the ability to see deals with wisdom and revelation. Eli's eyes got dim, because he got used to watching immorality in the house of God. He kept watching his sons sleep with the women of the church and take the offerings, and he never corrected this behavior. What this did was stifle his ability to see; that is, his ability to have wisdom, judgment and revelation. And this is what made him unable to raise up the Prophet Samuel. He needed eyes to be able to raise up a prophet, so Samuel had to be raised by God. What's amazing about this is Samuel was raised by God to be a seer, while being raised by someone who could not see. Moses, on the other hand, was a man of revelation. Moses was married to revelation because he was married to Jethro's oldest daughter, Zipporah. Jethro had seven daughters, all of whom corresponded with the seven creational days. On the first day of creation, God said, "Let there be light," which corresponds to the first daughter of Jethro. Of course, that is Zipporah. When Moses married Zipporah, he was marrying revelation. And when he slept with revelation or, better yet, created a baby with revelation, he birthed the first five books of the Bible.

Why didn't Moses eyes get dim? The Bible tells us that Moses went up the mountain and into the presence of the Lord, and when he came down, his face shined with light. His eyes, of course, were a part of his face. Moses' eyes never got dim because he stayed in the presence of the Lord. The reason Eli's eyes got dim was because he allowed his sons and Samuel to sleep in the presence of the Lord while he didn't do anything. When we deal with revelation, we're dealing with present truths and how to make the scriptures applicable to today's needs and demands. It's the Ramah Word of God (man shall not live by bread alone, but by every word that proceeds out of the mouth of God). When we talk about revelation, we're not just talking about what the Holy Spirit reveals from the scriptures, we're dealing with how God is specifically speaking to us individually. For example, what revelation do you get when you're reading the Word and God shows something to you; that is, when He shows you doing it, obeying it or implementing it? When you see yourself in the text, that text becomes revelation or Ramah to you.

First off, what is the purpose of revelation, and why do we need it? The Greek word for "revelation" is "apokalupsis," and it literally means:

- an unveiling
- an uncovering
- a revealing

What this tells us is that revelation is an introduction to a present truth that was once hidden; it is the opening of our eyes to see or understand something that we could not see or understand before.

Genesis 1:1-3
In the beginning God created the heaven and the earth. And the earth was without form, and void; and darkness was upon the face of the deep. And the Spirit of God moved upon the face of the waters. And God said, Let there be light: and there was light.

Genesis 1:1-3 gives us a snapshot of revelation. In the beginning, the Earth was without form and void. The word "void" means an empty space; it literally means absent of purpose. So, in the beginning, the Earth was absent of revelation because God hadn't spoken to it yet. He hadn't given it an assignment. But when He said, "Let there be light," He was literally speaking to the Earth's purpose. Of course, the light shined brightly, and the Earth waited for its next set

of instructions.

Genesis 2:7
And the LORD God formed man of the dust of the ground, and breathed into his nostrils the breath of life; and man became a living soul.

This is another picture of revelation. The minute Adam's eyes opened, he was greeted by revelation. This is what the scripture means when it says he became a living soul. The soul, of course, is comprised of the mind, will and emotions. Adam was a full-grown man when he was created; he was a perfect creation and a specimen of God. He knew what he needed to know, but his deity was limited by what he could not have (the knowledge of good and evil). He was to be lord over the Earth and everything in it, but Satan tempted his wife by telling her that they (she and Adam) could increase their rule as king and queen by tapping into spiritual matters that didn't concern them. Let's look at one more example of revelation.

Exodus 14:19-22
And the angel of God, which went before the camp of Israel, removed and went behind them; and the pillar of the cloud went from before their face, and stood behind them: And it came between the camp of the Egyptians and the camp of Israel; and it was a cloud and darkness to them, but it gave light by night to these: so that the one came not near the other all the night. And Moses stretched out his hand over the sea; and the LORD caused the sea to go back by a strong east wind all that night, and made the sea dry land, and the waters were divided. And the children of Israel went into the midst of the sea upon the dry ground: and the waters were a wall unto them on their right hand, and on their left.

Revelation was the light that illuminated the path for the Israelites; that same revelation could not be comprehended by the Egyptians, so it appeared as darkness to them. "That seeing they may see, and not perceive; and hearing they may hear, and not understand; lest at any time they should be converted, and their sins should be forgiven them" (Mark 4:12). All the same, the parting of the Red Sea represented another dimension of Revelation. The Israelites could see what they once could not see—a way out! Hear me—every season has a Genesis, and that season is not complete until there is a Revelation! This is why the Israelites ended up stuck in the wilderness (a place of disorder, perversion) for forty years when the Promised Land was just an eleven day journey from where they'd started! Their eyes had been darkened because of their rebellion! And God didn't give most of them the revelation they needed to enter into their next dimension of deliverance! God allowed Moses to see the Promised Land, but he was not allowed to enter it because of his rebellion (see Numbers 20:10-13).

Deuteronomy 34:1-5
And Moses went up from the plains of Moab unto the mountain of Nebo, to the top of Pisgah, that is over against Jericho. And the LORD shewed him all the land of Gilead, unto Dan, and all Naphtali, and the land of Ephraim, and Manasseh, and all the land of Judah, unto the utmost sea, And the south, and the plain of the valley of Jericho, the city of palm trees, unto Zoar. And the LORD said unto him, This is the land which I sware unto Abraham, unto Isaac, and unto Jacob, saying, I will give it unto thy seed: I have caused thee to see it with thine eyes, but thou shalt not go over thither. So Moses the servant of the LORD died there in the land of Moab, according to the word of the LORD.

Every generation needs revelation, and to get that revelation, every generation needs a revelator. When a generation has been blinded by a lack of leadership, bondage and perversion then spread like wildfire until they consume that generation. Thankfully, God stepped in and raised Samuel Himself because Eli's eyes had been dimmed by what he chose not to see. This is why we have been taxed with the responsibility to become uncompromising, God-fearing believers who can raise up the Eli's and lead them into revelation. In short, our job is open the eyes of the next generation before our natural eyes close. All the same, we have to follow and honor the leaders God has put in place to lead us from the wilderness to the revelation of who we are; this is so that when God calls our names, we'll know His voice and we'll answer the call the first time!

More Biblical Facts

The Bible contains 611,000 words	It takes around 90 hours to read the Bible in its entirety.	The Bible has been translated into 698 languages.
Methuselah was the oldest man to have lived in the Bible. He lived to be 969 years old.	Enoch and Eli are the two men in the Bible who did not die, but were instead, taken up to Heaven.	The Bible was written on three continents: Africa, Asia and Europe.
The Bible was written over a span of 1500 years.	The King James Bible contains 788,258 words.	The Bible mentions (by name) a total of 188 women.
The Old Testament took over 1500 years to write.	The Old Testament contains over 300 prophecies about Jesus that have been fulfilled.	The last word in the Bible is Amen.

Three Languages of the Bible		
Hebrew	Aramaic	Greek

Rivers Mentioned in the Bible

River	Scriptures
Abanah	2 Kings 5:12
Ahava	Ezra 8:21, 31
Arnon	Deuteronomy 2:24, 36, Joshua 12:2, Isaiah 16:2
Chebar (Kebar)	Ezekiel 1:1, 3, Ezekiel 3:15, 23, Ezekiel 10:15, 20, 22
Euphrates	Genesis 2:14, Joshua 1:4, Jeremiah 46:2, 6, 10
Gihon	Genesis 2:13
Habor	2 Kings 17:6, 2 Kings 18:11, 1 Chronicles 5:26
Jabbok	Deuteronomy 2:37, Deuteronomy 3:16, Joshua 12:2
Jordan	Joshua 3:8, 11, 13, 14, 15, Matthew 3:6, Mark 1:5
Kanah	Joshua 16:8, Joshua 17:9
Kishon	Judges 4:7, 13, Judges 5:21
Nile	Genesis 41:1, 3, 17, Exodus 2:3, Exodus 7:20-21
Pharpar	2 Kings 5:12
Pishon (Pison)	Genesis 2:11

River	Scriptures
Shihor (Sihor)	Joshua 13:3, Isaiah 23:3, Jeremiah 2:18
Tigris (Hiddekel)	Genesis 2:14, Daniel 10:4
Ulai	Daniel 8:2,16

The Garden of Eden

Four Rivers

River Name	Pishon	Gihon	Tigris	Euphrates
Meaning	Full Flowing	Bursting Forth	Swifting/Darting	Sweet/Fruitful

Genesis 2:10-14
And a river went out of Eden to water the garden; and from thence it was parted, and became into four heads. The name of the first is Pison: that is it which compasseth the whole land of Havilah, where there is gold; and the gold of that land is good: there is bdellium and the onyx stone. And the name of the second river is Gihon: the same is it that compasseth the whole land of Ethiopia. And the name of the third river is Hiddekel: that is it which goeth toward the east of Assyria. And the fourth river is Euphrates.

The Trees

There are two trees specifically named in the Bible.

Tree of Life	Tree of the Knowledge of Good and Evil

Genesis 2:8-9
And the LORD God planted a garden eastward in Eden; and there he put the man whom he had formed. And out of the ground made the LORD God to grow every tree that is pleasant to the sight, and good for food; the tree of life also in the midst of the garden, and the tree of knowledge of good and evil.

An Exegetical View of Eden's Trees

Some theologians argue that there were only two trees in the Garden of Eden, but as we can see in the aforementioned scripture, this is not true. Whenever you find yourself in a theological discussion, it is important that you are able to search out the scriptures and read the text in its entirety. And don't be rushed to give an answer! Rushed answers are oftentimes wrong, incomplete, without basis or emotionally driven. Please understand that over the course of your life, you will come across people who are more concerned with appearing to be intelligent as opposed to speaking truth. They've studied the Bible just so they can create a platform for themselves by arguing with you or anyone who professes to know the Bible! They are passionate about winning arguments, and they use emotional theatrics to accomplish their goal. This is why you first have to know what discussions to engage in, versus which ones to avoid. If you're not sure, follow this pattern:

1. Engage in theological discussions where the other party or parties involved are open to learning and embracing a perspective that is contrary to their own.
2. Avoid theological debates of any kind. If the other party or parties involved get loud, tries to draw a crowd, laughs or becomes argumentative, don't engage that person. Doing so would not edify the body of Christ. Remember, don't cast your pearls (wisdom) to swine (filthy flesh).
3. Avoid theological discussions where you have little to no knowledge on a specific subject. If you are engaging a person in an area where you are knowledgeable, and that person navigates to an area where you are weak, disengage. Point him or her to a person, a video or a book, and end that conversation.

Nevertheless, let's look at the Garden of Eden, and answer the question, "How many trees were in the Garden?" The purpose of this discussion is to teach you to take something as basic as this and pull the truth out of the scriptures. There were two trees mentioned because of their significance, but the text literally says, "And put of the ground made the Lord God to grow EVERY tree that is pleasant to the sight." This indicates that there were more than two trees. Let's look at another scripture to effectively establish this point.

Genesis 2:15-17
And the LORD God took the man, and put him into the garden of Eden to dress it and to keep it. And the LORD God commanded the man, saying, Of every tree of the garden thou mayest freely eat: But of the tree of the knowledge of good and evil, thou shalt not eat of it: for in the day that thou eatest thereof thou shalt surely die.

Genesis 3:1-3
Now the serpent was more subtil than any beast of the field which the LORD God had made. And he said unto the woman, Yea, hath God said, Ye shall not eat of every tree of the garden? And the woman said unto the serpent, We may eat of the fruit of the **trees** of the garden: But of the fruit of the tree which is in the midst of the garden, God hath said, Ye shall not eat of it, neither shall ye touch it, lest ye die.

Every type of tree that we see or read about today originated from the Garden of Eden. They weren't created in a vacuum, nor did they just start springing up! How do we know this? Genesis 1:11 confirms this truth; it reads, "And God said, Let the earth bring forth grass, the herb yielding seed, and the fruit tree yielding fruit after his kind, whose seed is in itself, upon the earth: and it was so."

Do you see how I came to this conclusion? First off, let me state this—a discussion as basic as this one should not stretch over thirty minutes. The more knowledgeable you have, the less time you'll spend proving an already established truth! Next, a biblical discussion should ALWAYS be centered around edification! Don't involve yourself in theological discussions or debates where God is not glorified.

Look at the Trees Again (An Allegorical Perspective)	
Tree of the Knowledge of Good and Evil	**Tree of Life**
Lucifer	Jesus Christ
Death	Everlasting Life
Darkness	Light
Blindness	Sight

Mark 8:22-25
And he cometh to Bethsaida; and they bring a blind man unto him, and besought him to touch him. And he took the blind man by the hand, and led him out of the town; and when he had spit on his eyes, and put his hands upon him, he asked him if he saw ought. And he looked up, and said, I see men as trees, walking. After that he put his hands again upon his eyes, and made him look up: and he was restored, and saw every man clearly.

Challenge
Based on the patterns of God, how many trees would you guess that are in the Garden of Eden? List your answer and argument below.

Your Answer

THE HISTORY OF THE BIBLE

The following timeline were taken from LearnReligions.com

Era	Description/Event
Creation - B.C. 2000	Originally, the earliest Scriptures are handed down from generation to generation orally.
Circa B.C. 2000-1500	The book of Job, perhaps the oldest book of the Bible, is written.
Circa B.C. 1500-1400	The stone tablets of the Ten Commandments are given to Moses at Mount Sinai and later stored in the Ark of the Covenant.
Circa B.C. 1400–400	The manuscripts comprising the original Hebrew Bible (39 Old Testament books) are completed. The Book of the Law is kept in the tabernacle and later in the Temple beside the Ark of the Covenant.
Circa B.C. 300	All of the original Old Testament Hebrew books have been written, collected, and recognized as official, canonical books.
Circa B.C. 250–200	The Septuagint, a popular Greek translation of the Hebrew Bible (39 Old Testament books), is produced. The 14 books of the Apocrypha are also included.
Circa A.D. 45–100	Original 27 books of the Greek New Testament are written.
Circa A.D. 140-150	Marcion of Sinope's heretical "New Testament" prompted Orthodox Christians to establish a New Testament canon.
Circa A.D. 200	The Jewish Mishnah, the Oral Torah, is first recorded.
Circa A.D. 240	Origen compiles the Hexapla, a six-columned parallel of Greek and Hebrew texts.
Circa A.D. 305-310	Lucian of Antioch's Greek New Testament text becomes the basis for the Textus Receptus.
Circa A.D. 312	Codex Vaticanus is possibly among the original 50 copies of the Bible ordered by Emperor Constantine. It is eventually kept in the Vatican Library in Rome.
A.D. 367	Athanasius of Alexandria identifies the complete New Testament canon (27 books) for the first time.
A.D. 382-	Saint Jerome translates the New Testament from original Greek into Latin. This

Era	Description/Event
384	translation becomes part of the Latin Vulgate manuscript.
A.D. 397	Third Synod of Carthage approves the New Testament canon (27 books).
A.D. 390-405	Saint Jerome translates the Hebrew Bible into Latin and completes the Latin Vulgate manuscript. It includes the 39 Old Testament books, 27 New Testament books, and 14 Apocrypha books.
A.D. 500	By now the Scriptures have been translated into multiple languages, not limited to but including an Egyptian version (Codex Alexandrinus), a Coptic version, an Ethiopic translation, a Gothic version (Codex Argenteus), and an Armenian version. Some consider the Armenian to be the most beautiful and accurate of all ancient translations.
A.D. 600	The Roman Catholic Church declares Latin as the only language for Scripture.
A.D. 680	Caedmon, English poet and monk, renders Bible books and stories into Anglo Saxon poetry and song.
A.D. 735	Bede, English historian and monk, translates the Gospels into Anglo Saxon.
A.D. 775	The Book of Kells, a richly decorated manuscript containing the Gospels and other writings, is completed by Celtic monks in Ireland.
Circa A.D. 865	Saints Cyril and Methodius begin translating the Bible into Old Church Slavonic.
A.D. 950	The Lindisfarne Gospels manuscript is translated into Old English.
Circa A.D. 995-1010	Aelfric, an English abbot, translates parts of Scripture into Old English.
A.D. 1205	Stephen Langton, theology professor and later Archbishop of Canterbury, creates the first chapter divisions in the books of the Bible.
A.D. 1229	Council of Toulouse strictly forbids and prohibits lay people from owning a Bible.
A.D. 1240	French Cardinal Hugh of Saint Cher publishes the first Latin Bible with the chapter divisions that still exist today.
A.D. 1325	English hermit and poet, Richard Rolle de Hampole, and English poet William Shoreham translate the Psalms into metrical verse.
Circa A.D. 1330	Rabbi Solomon ben Ismael first places chapter divisions in the margins of the Hebrew Bible.
A.D. 1381-1382	John Wycliffe and associates, in defiance of the organized Church, believing that people should be permitted to read the Bible in their own language, begin to translate and produce the first handwritten manuscripts of the entire Bible in

Era	Description/Event
	English. These include the 39 Old Testament books, 27 New Testament books, and 14 Apocrypha books.
A.D. 1388	John Purvey revises Wycliffe's Bible.
A.D. 1415	31 years after Wycliffe's death, the Council of Constance charges him with more than 260 counts of heresy.
A.D. 1428	44 years after Wycliffe's death, church officials dig up his bones, burn them, and scatter the ashes on Swift River.
A.D. 1455	After the invention of the printing press in Germany, Johannes Gutenberg produces the first printed Bible, the Gutenberg Bible, in the Latin Vulgate.
A.D. 1516	Desiderius Erasmus produces a Greek New Testament, a forerunner to the Textus Receptus.
A.D. 1517	Daniel Bomberg's Rabbinic Bible contains the first printed Hebrew version (Masoretic text) with chapter divisions.
A.D. 1522	Martin Luther translates and publishes the New Testament for the first time into German from the 1516 Erasmus version.
A.D. 1524	Bomberg prints a second edition Masoretic text prepared by Jacob ben Chayim.
A.D. 1525	William Tyndale produces the first translation of the New Testament from Greek into English.
A.D. 1527	Erasmus publishes a fourth edition Greek-Latin translation.
A.D. 1530	Jacques Lefèvre d'Étaples completes the first French language translation of the entire Bible.
A.D. 1535	Myles Coverdale's Bible completes Tyndale's work, producing the first complete printed Bible in the English language. It includes the 39 Old Testament books, 27 New Testament books, and 14 Apocrypha books.
A.D. 1536	Martin Luther translates the Old Testament into the commonly spoken dialect of the German people, completing his translation of the entire Bible in German.
A.D. 1536	Tyndale is condemned as a heretic, strangled, and burned at the stake.
A.D. 1537	The Matthew Bible (commonly known as the Matthew-Tyndale Bible), a second complete printed English translation, is published, combining the works of Tyndale, Coverdale and John Rogers.
A.D. 1539	The Great Bible, the first English Bible authorized for public use, is printed.
A.D. 1546	Roman Catholic Council of Trent declares the Vulgate as the exclusive Latin

Era	Description/Event
	authority for the Bible.
A.D. 1553	Robert Estienne publishes a French Bible with chapter and verse divisions. This system of numbering becomes widely accepted and is still found in most Bible's today.
A.D. 1560	The Geneva Bible is printed in Geneva, Switzerland. It is translated by English refugees and published by John Calvin's brother-in-law, William Whittingham. The Geneva Bible is the first English Bible to add numbered verses to the chapters. It becomes the Bible of the Protestant Reformation, more popular than the 1611 King James Version for decades after its original release.
A.D. 1568	The Bishop's Bible, a revision of the Great Bible, is introduced in England to compete with the popular but "inflammatory toward the institutional Church" Geneva Bible.
A.D. 1582	Dropping its 1,000-year-old Latin-only policy, the Church of Rome produces the first English Catholic Bible, the Rheims New Testament, from the Latin Vulgate.
A.D. 1592	The Clementine Vulgate (authorized by Pope Clementine VIII), a revised version of the Latin Vulgate, becomes the authoritative Bible of the Catholic Church.
A.D. 1609	The Douay Old Testament is translated into English by the Church of Rome, to complete the combined Douay-Rheims Version.
A.D. 1611	The King James Version, also called the "Authorized Version" of the Bible is published. It is said to be the most printed book in the history of the world, with more than one billion copies in print.
A.D. 1663	John Eliot's Algonquin Bible is the first Bible printed in America, not in English, but in the native Algonquin Indian language.
A.D. 1782	Robert Aitken's Bible is the first English language (KJV) Bible printed in America.
A.D. 1790	Matthew Carey publishes a Roman Catholic Douay-Rheims Version English Bible in America.
A.D. 1790	William Young prints the first pocket-sized "school edition" King James Version Bible in America.
A.D. 1791	The Isaac Collins Bible, the first family Bible (KJV), is printed in America.
A.D. 1791	Isaiah Thomas prints the first illustrated Bible (KJV) in America.
A.D. 1808	Jane Aitken (daughter of Robert Aitken), is the first woman to print a Bible.
A.D. 1833	Noah Webster, after publishing his famous dictionary, releases his own revised

Era	Description/Event
	edition of the King James Bible.
A.D. 1841	The English Hexapla New Testament, a comparison of the original Greek language and six important English translations, is produced.
A.D. 1844	The Codex Sinaiticus, a handwritten Koine Greek manuscript of both Old and New Testament texts dating back to the fourth century, is rediscovered by German Bible scholar Konstantin Von Tischendorf in the Monastery of Saint Catherine on Mount Sinai.
A.D. 1881-1885	The King James Bible is revised and published as the Revised Version (RV) in England.
A.D. 1901	The American Standard Version, the first major American revision of the King James Version, is published.
A.D. 1946-1952	The Revised Standard Version is published.
A.D. 1947-1956	The Dead Sea Scrolls are discovered.
A.D. 1971	The New American Standard Bible (NASB) is published.
A.D. 1973	The New International Version (NIV) is published.
A.D. 1982	The New King James Version (NKJV) is published.
A.D. 1986	The discovery of the Silver Scrolls, believed to be the oldest Bible text ever, is announced. They were found three years earlier in the Old City of Jerusalem by Gabriel Barkay of Tel Aviv University.
A.D. 1996	The New Living Translation (NLT) is published.
A.D. 2001	The English Standard Version (ESV) is published.

Major and Minor Prophets of the Bible

Amos
Daniel
Ezekiel
Habakkuk
Haggai
Hosea
Isaiah
Jeremiah
Joel
Jonah
Lamentations
Malachi
Micah
Nahum
Obadiah
Zechariah
Zephaniah

Old Testament Books (Second Half)

Amos
Daniel
Ecclesiastes
Ezekiel
Habakkuk
Haggai
Hosea
Isaiah
Jeremiah
Joel
Jonah
Lamentations
Micah
Nahum
Obadiah
Song of Solomon
Zechariah
Zephaniah
Malachi

Old Testament Books

Deuteronomy	Judges
Esther	Leviticus
Exodus	Nehemiah
Ezra	Numbers
First Chronicles	Proverbs
First Kings	Psalms
First Samuel	Ruth
Genesis	Second Chronicles
Job	Second Kings
Joshua	Second Samuel

Made in the USA
Las Vegas, NV
22 March 2021